Solovetski Patericon

The Holy Fathers of the Solovetski Isles

Gozalov Books
The Hague

© Gozalov Books, The Hague, 2023
Publisher: Marijcke Tooneman
Telephone: +31703521565
E-mail: gozalovbooks@planet.nl
Website: www.hetsmallepad.nl

ISBN: 9789079889785; 978-90-79889-78-5
The English translation of a Russian book ´Соловецкий Патерикон'

Editors: Convent of the Mother of God Portaïtissa, Trazegnies, Belgium, portaitissa@skynet.be;
Gouri Gozalov
Translator: Anna Dolgatcheva
Illustrations: Natalia Komarovskaya
Cover image: watercolor painting by Natalia Komarovskaya "Saints Sabbatios, Zosima and Herman"
Design: Guram Kochi

All rights reserved. No part of this publication may be reproduced or transmitted in any form or by any means, electronic or mechanical, including photocopy and recording, or stored in a retrieval system, without the written permission of the publisher.

†

*This book is published with the blessing of Monsignor
Simon, Archbishop of Brussels and Belgium*

Table of Contents

Foreword by the Publisher 6
Introduction 8
General history of the ascetics of the Solovetski Isles 26
Saint Sabbatios, Founder of Solovetski Ascetics and
Miracle-Worker 28
The Venerable hegumen Zosima, Miracle Worker of
Solovetski Isle 36
The Venerable Herman, Solovetski Miracle-Worker 48
The Venerable Elisha of Soumy 51
Blessed Theodoretos, missionary to the Lopars 56
The Venerable Hegumen Philip, the future Holy
Metropolitan of Moscow and all Russia 59
The Venerable John and Longin of Yarenga (+1561) 77
The Venerable Bassian and Jonah
of Pertominsk (+1561) 81
Hermits of the XVIIth century 85
The venerable Irenarch, hegumen of the Solovetsky
Monastery (+1628) 92
The venerable Eleazar, the founder of the Skete of the
Holy Trinity on Anzer 96
Hieroschemamonk Job, founder of the Golgotha-
Crucifixion Hermitage 123
Hermit Theophane 152
Starets Nahum 173
Hieromonk Matthew 193
Schemamonk Gerasim 196
The Monk Pamfilios 199
Schemamonk Zosima 201
Hieroschemamonk Jerome 203
Schemamonk Nikodemos 211
Schemamonk John 213
Schemamonk Theodore 215
Schemamonks Adam and Andrew 217
Schemamonks Hilarion and Matthew 218
The Monk Michael 219

Novice John Sorokin.. 221
Conclusion.. 224

Foreword by the Publisher

In the Christian tradition the Patericon is a collection of short stories which contains the description of the lives, spiritual practices and, sometimes, teachings of the Christian practitioners, monks or ascetics. Their experiences on the Path to finding God in their hearts has been a great help to thousands of practitioners who have followed the spiritual Path, strengthening their spirit, protecting them from dangers and helping them to see the next step on the Path.

Patericons were also a favourite reading for those worldly people who were concerned with the question of their posthumous fate, and who tried to remember God amidst their worldly pursuits.

Each Patericon describes the life and practices of a certain monastic community e.g. Synai Patericon, Egyptian Patericon or, later, the Kievski and Volocolamski Patericons.

The Solovetzki Patericon was published anonymously in 1873 in St. Petersburg. It tells us of the monks and hermits who lived and practised on the Solovetzki Isles in the White Sea, in the deep North of Russia. Solovetzki monasteries and hermitages, with regard to their spiritual achievements and influence on the Russian Orthodox Church, can be compared to the influence that the monasteries of the Athos mountain had on the Greek Orthodox Church. One of the examples is Saint Eleazar of Anzer, who founded the Trinity Hermitage of Anzer. He was the spiritual mentor of the future patriarch Nicon, who later reformed the entire Russian Orthodox Church.

A special feature of Solovetzki Patericon is that it also contains a description of the life of the monks and practitioners who humbly practised the Christian path all their lives and still did not achieve sanctity. These stories help to understand the depth of monastic life even more.

The reader will find interesting stories about the events in the lives of the monks which led them to spiritual illumination, or pointed out the path to further development of the soul.

Marijcke Tooneman

Introduction

The monastic life. Its meaning. Special features of the monastic life on the Solovetski Islands. Ordeals. The noviciate. Admittance to the monastic vows. Seclusion. Daily life. Matins. Liturgy. Refectory. Vespers. The Rule. The superior. The Cathedral. Duties. Services. The work of obedience. Death

The monastic life is according to its purpose an inner, concealed life. Although for a storyteller writing about life in a cloister, it would be exactly the external events which would draw his attention, for the cloister itself they are of minor importance as the main purpose of life for a monk, an ascetic, is the salvation of his soul. Things like struggling with external enemies, material achievements and an activity in the world for only earthly purposes are not important for monks. Their vocation is to struggle with the inner enemies of salvation, which takes place in the innermost depth of the soul; striving for better morality and, generally speaking, spiritual activity. The feats in this field are known mostly only to the Omniscient God.

In the early years of Christianity, the first monks' communities, which grew quickly in the deserts of Egypt, struck the world by their codes of life, which were completely opposite to those of life in the world. In those times many were collecting stories about the Christian ascetics and were writing their biographies. These biographies are the basis of the Historia Lausiaca and the Spiritual Meadow. People who went to visit hermits were pious men and women who looked for guidance in life and spiritual matters, and therefore they wrote down the instructive sayings of the holy fathers and their feats in the ascetic field.

Nowadays the monastic life is considered to be something quite normal. Many do not consider it a heroic deed to renounce family and public ties, all the pleasures of life and to lock oneself up between the walls of one or other monastery.

Solovetski Monastery. View from the south-east, from the Holy Lake

They do not see it as a merit that a monk spends the main part of his day busy with church services and prayers. An ordinary monk, who must obey without any contradiction the strict regulations of life in a monastery concerning the food and the will of the superior, and who is not capable of special zeal in ascetic practices, often passes away being completely unknown to anybody outside the monastery. Those who visit monasteries can gain an impression of the buildings and the church services, but the inner life of the monks remains unknown to them. The monks, in their turn, do not occupy themselves with the recording the events in their monastery, sometimes out of humility and sometimes because of the considerable work of obedience which consumes all their time. If each monastery would keep records about its remarkable monks and these records would be preserved in the monastery's archives then the list of ascetics would be longer and people would have a better, more objective knowledge of the monastic life.

View of the Solovetski monastery from the Tsar's Pier

If we take the life of a Solovetski monk from his entering the monastery to his death, we can see that his life in itself is a heroic deed. Only a sincere and firm determination to serve God for the salvation of one's soul can prompt one to look for a place in the monastery of Solovetski Island. This island is located in the White Sea at a distance of about forty five kilometres from the shore. The sea is covered with ice for eight months a year. The vegetation on the island is poor, and the eight months long, dark winter is foggy and humid. The only advantage of the island is solitude and remoteness from the rest of the world. Taking this into account, it would be quite natural to think that the determination to live on such an island would be enough to prove one's sincere wish to lead a monastic life. But in fact no aspirant is accepted as a novice directly. Everyone who wishes to join the monastery lives at first for a year with the pilgrims. Every year about three hundred pilgrims stay in the monastery. They lodge in the three buildings outside the cloister or, if there is need for it, they lodge inside the cloister, in its various workshops. The aspirant, accomplishing during the probation year various works of obedience, has enough time and opportunity to think about whether he is capable of leading a monastic life, to become acquainted with the monks and to find his spiritual mentor, to whom he could entrust himself and by whom he could be guided in his spiritual life. If after one year his determination remains unchanged then the monastery's authorities keep an eye on him even more attentively and only after a couple more years he may hope to be accepted officially as a novice.

None of the aspirants enjoy privileges: all of them share the same food and all of them eat together in a refectory separately from the monks. They live in big common rooms, wear the same clothes and must do the work of obedience. The only thing which is taken into account by the monks who share out the work, is the physical strength of the aspirants, and the weakest ones get the lightest jobs. This regulation has at least two useful results: on the one hand, it soon becomes clear, through the work of obedience, who has a tendency to self-will or is superficial, and, therefore, not eligible for the monastic life. On the other hand, the work of obedience, which is something that the aspirant should perform whether he likes it or not, and which is not always pleasant, teaches him to reason humbly, and to be obedient and patient. All the ascetics who use the lessons of their noviciate to their advantage, remember this period with emotion. It takes a long time before the novice receives a cell of his own and it takes even longer before he will be allowed to make his monastic vows. A novice must acquire it by long feats of piety and hard work and therefore he accepts it (the vow) gladly and joyfully. Only a few receive the monk's mantya sooner than ten years after joining the monastery. The day he makes his vows is then a day of spiritual celebration for both the new monk and for the monks, who witness a true servant of God taking his place in their ranks! How could he not rejoice, when his innermost wishes become fulfilled after many years of efforts! The heart of an observer from the outside world would hardly be able not to feel emotion by the touching ceremony of the consecration, when the novice renounces the world and all its passions, takes on himself the saving yoke of Christ by the vows of chastity, poverty and obedience. As a newborn baby after baptism is entrusted to his godfather to be brought up in a spirit of faith and piety, so the new monk is entrusted before the altar and the Gospel, which symbolizes Christ Himself, like a son to his spiritual father who will teach him the ascetic life.

The life of a monk flows quietly and placidly year after year, along the path of the cross that he has chosen, to the last threshold, common to all people. From the very day of his consecration the indispensable fulfilling of these vows, for which he has been schooling himself since he joined the monastery will start. Especially the vow of obedience will govern all the thoughts, the entire soul and bodily energy of a Solovetski monk until the end of his days. This is the reason why the major part of the monks on the Solovetski Isles find rest only when they are either seriously ill and cannot get out of bed, or in the grave. Holy orders and various monastery posts are accepted by the monks only as a work of obedience. Only a few, after saying farewell to the world forever, will visit the mainland again, when the needs of the community compel one or other monk to leave the monastery for a while.

The great monastic vow is made only by aged monks, who become exhausted from their work or who are terminally ill. However, the great-schema[1] monks, these hermits within the monastery, keep themselves busy with one or other work because of their zeal: e.g. one will wear spectacles for his weak eyes and sew; another will net the new nets or undo the old ones; the most feeble pick at old ropes to make the material for the caulking of the boats.

The daily life of a Solovetski monk from the very moment when the bell sounds, breaking the night stillness, calling for morning prayers, is a constant succession of work and prayer.

The night in the monastery, completely surrounded by high walls, feels majestic. Silence reigns everywhere, deep darkness, in which there twinkles, like a cherished star, the little flame of the inextinguishable oil lamp before the icon of the Mother of God, which was once damaged by an enemy bullet.

After midnight, one hour before the ringing of the church bells, one hears along the walls and in the corridors the rapid ringing of the small bell to wake the brethren, a kind of archangel's trumpet, which will wake up the dead at the Last Judgment.

---

[1] The monastic vow and also the name of the cloth worn by the schemamonk. There are the small and the great schema. It is also called 'the great angelic vow'.

Two schemamonks

The activities in the monastery do not start directly after the ringing of the bell, because the monks getting up after a short rest from the work of the previous day, fulfil their prayer rule and dedicate to God their first thoughts and feelings on the new day. On weekdays the morning service starts at three a.m., and on feasts it starts at two or one a.m. Shortly before the ringing of the church bells, monks come from all parts of the monastery, making their way mostly to the church of Saints Zosima and Sabbatios as it is the custom of the monastery that every monk must bow first before the wonder-working relics of the Saints and ask their blessing and support for their daily work.

The monks who have certain works of obedience to do, then mostly remain in this church for the Midnight Service. The superior and all the priests however, except those who work in the hospital, celebrate the service in the main cathedral of the monastery. Everyone should be at the service: therefore the brother who rings the first bell, at the very beginning of the midnight service, having first prayed before the principal icons and having received the blessing of the superior, checks whether all the monks are present: he starts on the kliros and then he walks all round the church. If he notices that some monks are absent, he goes and wakes them up again. If they still don't come, he reports it to the superior, explaining the reason of their absence. After the 'The Lord is God' and the troparion are sung, the head of the bakery and the kitchen, bows before the principal icons and receives the blessing of the superior for his work. He lights a candle from the oil lamp, which burns before the main icon of the cathedral, and uses this flame to light the stoves in the kitchen.

The interior of the cathedral of the Holy Trinity (built 1862)

The monks, the novices and the pilgrims leave the church and start their daily work of obedience, which lasts the whole day. Only the priests, the oldest monks and the brethren of the hospital continue the service. The oldest monks however may only be present if they do not fail in their duties.

The service in the cathedral is longer than in other churches: all the stichiras and kathismas are sung slowly. During Matins, after the kathismas of the psalms, follow two or three readings: on weekdays the commentary of the blessed Theofilact the Bulgarian on the Gospel of the day; during Great Lent readings from Saint Ephrem the Syrian; during cheese-fare week and the week of the passion from the collection; on feast days the readings are taken from the works of different holy fathers. For the Service of the Hours during Great Lent the readings are taken from St John of the Ladder. On weekdays, the Matins last about three hours. During Great Lent, after the Matins there is a Panychida for the deceased brethren.

After Matins three or five early liturgies are celebrated, one after another. A lover of prayers and melodies could enjoy this from midnight until the afternoon. The last liturgy takes place at nine o'clock in the evening, and the superior and all the priests are present without any exception. During Matins and Vespers as well as during Liturgy prayers are always said for the repose of all deceased fathers and brothers and all the philanthropists who have helped the monastery, all whose names are recorded in the synodicon.

This commemoration is performed by hieromonks and the most devout monks. In the cathedral this pious duty is performed by four elders; in the other monastery and hermitage churches it is done by one elder. At the end of the Divine Liturgy the hieromonk sprinkles the tables in the refectory and all the food in the kitchen with blessed water; in the same way he blesses the dough and flour for use the next day in the bakery and prosphora[2] bakery. After the late Liturgy, during dinner, the Panagia prayer rule is performed daily. <u>Members of the</u> choir follow the canonarch who

---

2 A small bread stamped with a seal and used for the Communion or in memory of the living and the dead.

reads aloud Psalm 144, and walk from the cathedral to the refectory, they are followed by the hieromonk who carries on a dish a big prosphora prepared in honour of the Most Holy Mother of God; the Superior with the brethren who follow him close this ceremonial procession. Before dinner the brethren sing the Lord's prayer, and then the Superior, or, if he is absent, a hieromonk, blesses the prepared food and drink. Before eating, half of the prosphora of the Mother of God is cut up and passed around. The brethren's dinner always consists of four dishes, among which, on ordinary days, when there is no fast, salted cod predominates, a dish not much liked by those who are not accustomed to it, but which is the best food given to the coastal inhabitants by Divine Providence and which forms the basis of their nourishment and health. In summer they catch a lot of herring in the sea and make soup of it; in December and January they catch small fish under the ice. Numerous lakes on the islands, however, have hardly any fish, so the most frequent dish on the brethren's table is soup made of dry cod and flour. Desert is usually milk porridge; on feasts wheat bread is given instead. Lenten fare consists of mushrooms, berries and vegetables that grow on the islands. The monks' meals are solemn and this affects both the mind and the heart. The refectory is situated near the Cathedral of the Dormition of the Most Holy Mother of God; its walls and vaults are decorated with colossal pictures of the Lord's Passion, Gospel scenes and saints; about 400 monks and novices sit at long tables. The monks eat in silence; only the loud voice of the reader is heard, reading about the virtues and feats of the saint of the day, or useful admonitions of the silver-tongued Ephrem the Syrian, to encourage temperance and repentance. After dinner the offering of the panagia is performed according to the rule; this is accompanied by the singing of hymns. After the meal, the monks return to their work of obedience. Wine is never served at table; only for feasts the eldest brethren are allowed to have some wine in the cellarer's cell with the Superior's blessing; on great feasts they have wine in the Superior's rooms. The cold climate, long winters, fog, heavy sea winds, salty food and unceasing labour which exhaust the body, all these conditions excuse such leniency to human frailty.

The refectory

At 4 p.m. two early Vespers are held one after another; the church bell rings for the late Vespers at 6 p.m. and in winter at 5 p.m. after the end of all obedience work, so that all monks and pilgrims who laboured during the day can take part in the evening service. At Compline, according to monastic custom, the following canons are read: the Canon to the Sweetest Jesus, the Canon to the Mother of

God and the Guardian Angel, as well as the Akathist to the Saviour or the Mother of God. Compline is followed by supper consisting of three dishes, and after supper the brethren stay in the refectory and listen to the evening prayers. All Divine Services are performed with proper veneration and without any haste, so even on ordinary days all church services taken together last seven or eight hours.

The monk's prayer rule which in some monasteries is performed in church, is done in the Solovetsky Monastery, just like on Athos, by every monk in his own cell. Pilgrims can attend evening prayers with monks, and in summer all visitors may join them, but one cannot lay the same burden on them as on monks. Besides prostrations and the prayer of the Heart, each monk and novice must read daily a certain number of kathismas and commemorate both living and dead brethren and relatives at each "Glory to..."; some monks have the habit of reading several chapters of the Gospel and the Apostle as well as various canons and akathists. The amount, duration and time of the cell prayer rule depend on the ascetic's zeal and aspiration to God as well as on his spiritual father's will and directions.

The monks of Solovetsky perform many kinds of obedience work along with spiritual practice. The location of the Solovetsky Monastery on a secluded and barren island, surrounded by the sea and the sparsely populated and unproductive Pomorye, far from market towns, makes the monks produce almost all they need themselves. They neither sow nor reap, for the conditions they live under have given them many other and harder occupations. We will list the types of monastic obedience work in order to give you a better idea about life and work in the monastery.

The first kind of obedience work is the position of Superior which is always assumed by an archimandrite chosen by the Holy Synod among superiors and brethren of other monasteries, where he has already proved to have the appropriate abilities and to be worthy of the entrusted position. The Superior is the father, the head and the leader of his large family which consists of people who, in spite of the fact that they are strangers to each other and differ in rank, character, age and background, have entrusted themselves for the sake of God and their own salvation, to his fatherly guidance and have made it a rule to follow their father's will instead of their own. The Superior is in charge of the whole monastery; everything depends on him; both great and small things are done according to his orders and directions; everybody turns to him for advice and instructions concerning all monastic activities, and all his words and precepts are accepted with childlike trust, without any discussion or questions.

Therefore the Superior should have a strong and elevated spirit, a good knowledge of holy Scripture and the Fathers' works, as well as monastic rules, be the most skillful in monastic life and be noted for wisdom and experience. The lot of the Superior is difficult and hard. It is small wonder that many monks who have tasted the sweetness of the silent cell and dependent life look at the height of this rank with fear and do their best to avoid such a hard and burdensome cross.

The position of Superior is followed by the obedience's of prior, treasurer, magistrate, sacristan and confessor. For all these positions the Superior elects elder hieromonks who are intelligent and mature; they are then officially appointed to their positions by decrees of the Holy Synod in Moscow. The monks holding these positions, together with the Superior constitute the monastery synod; they are called the synod elders and have official meetings. This synod with the Superior at the head deals with all matters concerning the monastery management.

Church of Saint Philip, Metropolitan of Russia

The prior is the main assistant of the Superior and he is responsible for the monastery's economy.

The treasurer is in charge of money and all household items and materials.

The magistrate supervises brethren and pilgrims in the church, refectory and cells.

The sacristan is in charge of all church property, he looks after the cleanliness and order in the churches and sees to it that all church services are held on time and properly.

The confessor hears the confessions of the brethren during Lent. He is a spiritual doctor and teacher who teaches his children the spiritual life; therefore his cell is open day and night for anyone who may need instruction or admonition, who is bewildered, has inner conflicts and the various temptations that every ascetic encounters in his life. In summer he is given an assistant to confess visitors.

The next kind of obedience work is the celebration of church services; this is done by hieromonks and hierodeacons for periods of six weeks. All hieromonks and hierodeacons, except those engaged in secretarial work, painting, gold-plating, etc., are exempt from general obedience work and must attend all church services and zealously and diligently read Holy Scripture and other edifying books in their cells. Only sometimes the Superior may send hieromonks and hierodeacons to catch fish, stack hay and gather berries and mushrooms.

There is also the position of a rule-keeper to which a hieromonk or a hierodeacon who knows the church rules and choral singing to perfection is appointed. Each choir consists of a first singer, and other monks who have a talent for singing. There are also readers, canonarkhs, sextons and a monk who rings the bell to wake the brethren.

Except for this kind of church work there are other monastery positions and occupations: a librarian, a secretary of the synod, secretaries for the correspondence, bell ringers, buyers, a household manager, a cellarer, a keeper of the wardrobe, a barn-keeper, a skipper and mechanics (appointed upon examination), painters, lithographers, gold and silversmiths, gilders, carvers, stone cutters and polishers, watchmakers, candle-makers, cloth and linen dyers, coopers, metalworkers, prosphora-bakers, bakers, bookbinders, package-makers, joiners, yeast-makers, cart-makers, sledge-makers, wheelmen, carpenters, house painters, glass-cutters, fishermen, smiths, tailors, shoemakers, tanners, harness-makers, rope-makers, spinners, net-makers, fullers, stonemasons, bricklayers, stove-makers, plasterers, sailors, firemen, millers, malt makers, tallow-makers, woodcutters, vegetable gardeners, innkeepers, refectory workers, cooks, kvass-makers, laundrymen, trappers, tar extractors, coalmen, wood-carriers, grooms, cattle-farm workers, shepherds and other unskilled labourers. The brethren of the Solovetsky Monastery manage to satisfy most of theirs needs themselves. Each kind of work is called an obedience. In each kind of obedience the eldest and the most experienced monk is the head and manages the work entrusted to him and the workers; he is responsible to the prior and the manager of the household. Some kinds of obedience work are done by many people, for example, about seventy people work in the tailor's and the shoemaker's workshop; there are about sixty people who work on ships, schooners and boats; in winter thirty boys spin hemp for fishing nets and seines; about forty people, especially in summer, are engaged in fishing; sometimes about ten people work at the smithy. Many people, including the Superior, take part in haymaking. It is very important that everybody should have some work to do and it is even more important that nobody does anything without permission. There is a pious custom before manual work : this begins with a prayer to God and then, if the work is done with other monks, the head is asked: "Bless, father" and having received the answer: "God will bless", one crosses oneself and starts working praying the Jesus prayer, as if before the face of God Himself and under His almighty guidance and help.

Blessed are the monks who, according to the monastery rules have renounced their will and, with implicit obedience and evangelical self-denial, live in unceasing labour and constant prayer. They do not expect any rewards on earth for their feats. When a monk dies, three strokes of the big bell announce the death to the brethren; he is wrapped in his mantya and transferred to the church where the Psalter (or Gospel for a priest or deacon) is read till the burial service. After the service the brethren give the deceased the last kiss and carry him to the cemetery where he is put into a grave to the loud ringing of the bells which expresses the joy of the Church that a monk has finished his journey and is going to his rest. After that the brethren return to the church, where the last Litya is held over the kolyva[3], and then the Superior and all the monks make twelve prostrations singing: "Give rest, Lord, to the soul of Your departed servant". This canon should be performed by every monk for forty days. The name of the deceased is added to the church synodicon to be commemorated, and every monk includes it in the list of brethren to be commemorated during his cell prayers. A big wooden cross is erected over each grave to symbolize that the deceased carried his cross from his birth to his death, that he was a true follower of the Divine Cross-bearer and has gone from the earthly to the eternal life in the hope of his Redeemer and Saviour.

---

[3] A sweet dish made of grain and honey in memory of the departed

General history of the ascetics of the Solovetski Isles

The three Saints Father Sabbatios, Father Zosima and Father Herman shine like the resplendent stars amongst the Solovetski ascetics and Saints. They are the founders and the leaders of their monastery; they were the first inhabitants of the deserted Solovetski Isles, who poured the bright light of faith and piety upon the entire north of our fatherland. Their feats are inscribed forever in the history of the Solovetski Isles and the Orthodox Church holds sacred their memory. Their example inspired many monks, who were looking for a life of silent seclusion in the far north, amidst the harsh conditions of life which were in this case most favourable for ascetic practices. Thus the monks' life flourished on the Solovetski Isles and the monastery of Saint Sabbatios, Saint Zosima and Saint Herman has bred many ascetics who were worthy of being remembered by future generations. The influence of these three great men was very beneficial for their surroundings and their life remains instructive for everyone.

Besides the ascetics who reached sanctity in the Solovetski monastery, there were several members of the high clergy of the Russian Church who took their monastic vows and grew there spiritually. These were the Patriarchs Joasaf the First and Nikon; Metropolitans Isidore of Novgorod, Hilarion of Pskov, Ignatios of Tobolsk, Raphael of Astrakhan, Job of Novgorod; Archbishops Marcel of Vologda and Barsanuphios of Archangelsk. Patriarch Nikon, who greatly influenced the life of the entire Russian Church, made his monastic vow in the presence of Saint Eleazar, who was the founder of the Anzerski Hermitage. This remote monastery saw the first of

Nikon's severe ascetic feats. For four years Nikon had been maturing there and preparing himself for the future great work of governing of the Church, and it was there that he learned the patience that he would need when his fate would change. Thus the spiritual influence of the Solovetski monastery is not limited to its nearest surroundings only, but has spread all over Russia.

Saint Sabbatios, Founder of Solovetski Ascetics and Miracle-Worker

Life in the Cyrillo-Beloyezerski Monastery. Moving to Valaam Monastery. Meeting with Herman. Arriving on Solovetski Isle. A forecasting Sign. Presentiment of the End. Setting Sail for the river Vyga. Meeting with hegumen Nathanael. Communion. Conversation with John. Death and Burial. Translation of his Relics. Glorification

The first place of Saint Sabbatios' feats was the Cyrillo-Beloyezerski Monastery. Spending his time zealously in fasting, vigil and prayers, he was an example for all the monks. His obedience to the superior and brethren and his diligent carrying out of various tasks in the monastery, made those who knew him love and respect him. However, the humble monk did not want to be praised by his fellow men, and planned to retire to a secluded place. He heard a rumour that on the Isle of Valaam in the Ladoga Lake, there was a secluded monastery of the Transfiguration of the Lord, where the monks managed to find the necessary means to live solely by their own work, and where they distinguished themselves by the particular strictness of their ascetic rule. Sabbatios asked his superior and brethren to let him follow the call of his heart and go to that monastery. He received their blessing and he moved off to the Monastery of Valaam. However, his meek soul could not find rest there either. He soon excelled his new brethren by his feats and again his fame and the admiration of his fellow ascetics were his lot.

Sabbatios began to look for another, even more secluded place. His soul, which loved most of all a life in seclusion, rejoiced when he got to know that there was in the Far North of Russia, an isle in the sea, situated quite far from the continent. The superior of the Transfiguration Monastery and the brethren loved Sabbatios and did not want to be deprived of his presence so they pleaded him not to leave them. Sabbatios remained with them for a while, but he could not overcome the secret desire of his spirit. Once, deep in the night, he prayed to God and secretly left the monastery and started off for the Solovetski Isle.

After reaching the shore, he obtained from the local inhabitants detailed information about his destination. The isle, he was told, was far from the shore, and the journey there was dangerous as the sea was often stormy. It had about a hundred and six kilometres in circumference, and it had lakes with sweet water and fish, mountains and forests. However it still remained deserted because of the difficulties of communication with the mainland. The fishermen sometimes visited it, but after their work was done they left the isle again. These stories made Sabbatios' spirit even more enthusiastic as he realized that exactly there, on the Solovetski Isle, he would find the desired silence and solitude.

Having understood the monk's intention, the local inhabitants vividly described the inconveniences of life on a deserted island: 'What will you eat there and where will you get your clothes from? How can you live so far away from people?'

The starets[4] however placed all his hopes in God. Soon Providence led him to his future fellow-ascetic. Having come to the mouth of the river Vyga, Sabbatios found a monk called Herman, who lived there near the chapel. Herman confirmed all the <u>stories that the</u> starets had heard from the locals.

4 an older, wise monk, a spiritual mentor

St. Sabbatios

Sabbatios and Herman decided to sail to the isle and live there together. They found a boat and stocked food and the tools they would need when living in a deserted place. Their journey was without problems: obviously God blessed the monks' intention. What a joy they felt when they saw the isle, and what a delight when they stepped on land! At a distance of about 1,3 km from the shore, near a lake, they found a place that seemed suitable to settle. They erected a big wooden cross on the spot, built a hut near it to live in. Obtaining a poor sustenance by the work of their hands, they spent almost all their time praying and glorifying God.

For their consolation, God had shown them by a special sign the hidden predestination of the Solovetski Isle. The coastal inhabitants of the continent started to envy the monks, as they considered themselves to be the owners of the entire coastline and all the islands of the White Sea. So a fisherman with his wife and all his family, following the decision of the community, moved off to the isle and settled not far from the hut of Sabbatios and Herman. These kept their way of life unchanged. Once on Sunday, early in the morning, having finished his cell rule[5], Sabbatios went out of the hut with a censer in order to venerate the cross, and he heard loud crying, which resembled the cries of someone undergoing a flogging. Horrified, as he thought it was a delusion to tempt him, the Saint returned to his hut and told Herman about the cries. When Herman went out of the hut he also heard moans and shouting and he went in the direction where they were coming from. He soon found a sobbing woman who told him the following: "When I went to the lake to meet my husband there appeared two young men, shining with light. They caught me and flogged me with sticks saying at the same time: 'Go away from this place! You are not allowed to live here as according to God's will this place is meant for the monks only.' After this the men became invisible.' Herman returned to their hut and told Sabbatios what he had heard from the woman,

5 each monk is given certain prayers to say each day, this is called his cell rule.

and both of them glorified God. Meanwhile the
fisherman who was terrified by this vision, gathered
all his belongings and together with wife and family
returned to his village. From that moment none of
the secular people dared to settle on the deserted
isle.

For several years Sabbatios and Herman lived
on the isle in solitude. Sabbatios' soul had found
there the quiet and silence to which it had aspired
so firmly and constantly. When Herman set sail
to the river Onega to fetch some food and things
they needed, Starets Sabbatios remained on the
isle completely alone, before the countenance of
the omniscient God, Who watched his patience, his
praying labour and his spiritual feats. Comforted
by the visits of holy angels, Sabbatios practised
constant meditation of God and day by day he was
becoming still more prepared to enter eternity.

Having a premonition of his coming end, Starets
Sabbatios conceived a wish to receive Communion.
He got in a small boat and sailed to the shore.
After two days sailing, he reached the dry land and
headed for the chapel on the bank of the river Vyga.
At that time hegumen Nathanael was there to visit
the Orthodox Christians. According to God's will,
Father Nathanael, who was taking Communion to a
sick man, on his way met the Solovetski hermit. This
meeting rejoiced both of them: Starets Sabbatios
felt consoled as he found what he was longing
for, and Father Nathanael looked with delight at
Sabbatios' ascetic face, about whom he had heard
so much. 'Father,' Sabbatios said, 'forgive the sins
that I will confess to you, by the power given to
you by God, and let me receive the holy Eucharist.
For a long time I have wished to delight my soul
with this Divine food. Sustain me with It now. It
was Christ God who sent you to me to purify me
from all the sins I have committed in my entire life,

in word, in deed and in thought.' After confession Nathanael said: "God will forgive you, brother." Then he paused for a while and with tears in his eyes, and amazement, he said: "Oh Venerated one, how I wish that I only had your sins!"

Sabbatios answered: "The end of my life has come. I beseech you, let me receive the Divine Communion immediately." Hegumen Nathanael suggested that the Starets should go to the chapel and wait for him there, till he returned from the sick person, and then he would give him Communion. "Father", said Sabbatios to this, "do not postpone it till tomorrow. We do not know for sure whether we will live until the end of the day. How can we possibly know what will happen tomorrow?"

Fulfilling the Starets's wish, Father Nathanael gave him the Communion, and having kissed him brotherly, he asked Sabbatios to wait for him in the chapel until he returned. The Starets prayed diligently for a long time in the chapel, and then he entered a small cell and started to prepare himself to leave this life.

At that very moment a Novgorodian merchant, called John, who sailed on the Vyga with his goods, put in to the bank near the chapel. He entered the cell and found Sabbatios there, who started a conversation with him and told him about the love of poverty, charity and other good deeds. John offered Sabbatios some money and food, but Sabbatios did not want to take anything. He said to John: 'My son, stay here until the morning and you will witness God's grace and then you can sail further safely. John did not want to wait until the next day and he intended to continue his journey. But suddenly a storm started that caused big waves in the river and in the sea. The merchant, though against his will, had to stay there for the night. In the morning the wind subsided and John came to the cell in order to receive the farewell blessing from the Starets. He said the prayer (according to the custom) and knocked at the door but there was no answer. He entered the cell and he found Sabbatios sitting in his monks' habit and the censer standing near him. John said: 'Forgive me, God's servant that I entered your cell. Please give me your blessing so that I can safely continue my way.' There was no answer. John thought that Sabbatios was sleeping. He came up to him and touched him and only then did he realize that his holy soul had flown up to the Heavenly Father.

At that moment hegumen Nathanael returned from visiting the sick person, and seeing Sabbatios passed away already, he kissed his honourable head, with tears in his eyes. Both, Nathanael and John, told each other with amazement all that had happened: how Nathanael was chosen by Providence to give Communion to Sabbatios, and how John was also chosen by Providence to be worthy of listening to the last admonitions of Starets Sabbatios. His death took place on the 27th September 1435. Father Nathanael and the merchant John held the burial service according to the church rite and then they buried the honourable body of the Venerated Sabbatios. His relics were transferred to the Solovetski Monastery in the time of the Venerated hegumen Zosima and they were buried behind the altar of the Cathedral of the Dormition, where they remained until 1566. On the 8th August of that year his relics together with the relics of the Venerated Zosima were moved to the Cathedral's annex, which was built in the name of these two Miracle Workers.

During the Moscow assembly of 1547, in the days of Metropolitan Macarios, it was decided to celebrate the memory of the Venerated Sabbatios on the 27th September.

Nowadays his relics lie in the church of Saints Zosima and Sabbatios in a richly decorated shrine.

The Venerable hegumen Zosima, Miracle Worker of Solovetski Isle

*His origin. Secret aspiration to the monastic life.
Meeting with Herman. Arrival at Solovetski Isle.
Vision. Building the Monastery. Lonely winter.
Miraculous help. Construction of the Church of the
Transfiguration. Superiors Paul and Theodose.
Hegumen Zosima. The miracle with the prosfora.
Growth of the Monastery. Transfer of the relics of the
venerated Sabbatios. Harassments by the inhabitants
of the coast. Zosima's journey to Novgorod.
A prophesy and a vision. Last conversations.
Appointment of Superior. Death. Burial service.
Glorification*

A year after the death of Starets Sabbatios there appeared on the deserted Solovetski Isle a successor of his ascetics feats, a monk called Zosima. The Venerated Sabbatios can be called the founder of the ascetic life on Solovetski, as he was the first monk who lived on this isle fasting and praying. Zosima can be acknowledged as the founder and leader of the Solovetski Monastery.

Zosima came from the village of Tolvui in the Novgorod region, near lake Onega. His parents, Gabriel and Barbara, brought their son up in piety and love of what is good. From a young age Zosima was quiet, silent and meek. When he learned reading he liked mostly to read pious books. When he came of age, he did not want to marry, but, following his secret wish, he left his parents, put on black clothes and settled in a deserted place.

St Herman and St. Zosima

There Zosima, like a hermit, lived in prayer, fasting and meditating on God. Soon Providence showed him the way. Zosima became acquainted with a monk named Herman, who used to live with Starets Sabbatios on Solovetski Isle. Herman told Zosima that that isle, with its forests and lakes, is perfectly suitable for the monastic, ascetic life. The young hermit Zosima conceived a wish to follow Sabbatios in his ascetic feats and he asked Herman to take him to the Solovetski Isle. By that time Zosima's parents had died. He buried them and gave all their possessions to the poor. Then Herman and Zosima started for the isle. Their journey was without difficulties and they put in to the isle in the neighbourhood of a lake. They built a hut of tree branches and held a vigil, pleading God to bless their undertaking. The Lord encouraged them with a prophesying vision: when in the morning Zosima came out of their hut he saw an immaterial light which illuminated the entire area, and in the east he saw a beautiful church high in the air. Astounded he returned to the hut. Herman noticed a strange expression on Zosima's face and asked him about it. Having heard about his vision, he told Zosima about the miraculous driving away of the fisherman and about the prophesy that monks would live here. Herman concluded: 'Do not be afraid and listen attentively: it seems to me that God through you will gather many monks on this island.' Herman's story quietened Zosima and they decided to build a monastery. They prayed to God and started to cut wood in the forest and built a fence and some cells. They tilled the soil and grew vegetables and grain. However this bodily work did not weaken their prayer practice.

The hermits however, still had to undergo many ordeals before their dwelling became populated by monks. Herman went to the continent and lingered there. When he decided to sail for the isle, he could not do so because of the autumn storms which had driven a lot of ice to the shore so that the communication with the isle was cut off. Thus Herman stayed for the winter on the continent, and Zosima was alone on the island. Only God, Who knows the innermost and the secrets of a human being, knew the work and the feats of Zosima during that winter. He felt fortified by an unshakable hope in God, to Whom he had 'been holden up from the womb: thou art he that took me out of my mother's bowels' (Ps. 70, 6). Zosima underwent many temptations from the hater of all good, the evil spirit, which tried to frighten him by many apparitions. The manly warrior of Christ protected himself by the cross and prayers, and all the enemy's efforts remained idle.

In addition to this spiritual struggle there were worries about the daily bread in such a remote, deserted place. The winter was long and stern and the stock of food that they prepared during summer had run out. Zosima had no idea how to live to the end of the winter and sometimes the thought disturbed him that he might die of hunger. However, he did not give in to depression and consoled himself, trusting in Providence which had been benevolent to him so many times before. And the Lord soon helped his ascetic. Two strangers came to him once and gave him a stock of bread, flour and oil. They told Zosima: 'Please, father, this is for you. And if the Lord orders us, we will come to you again.' Zosima was so astounded he did not even ask them who they were. The strangers left and he never saw them again. It was clear to Zosima that God had visited him and that Providence guarded the chosen one.

When the winter was over, Herman came back to the island accompanied by a fisherman called Mark. Mark wanted to share the solitary life of the ascetics. Herman brought a sufficient stock of food and nets for fishing with him. Soon after, Mark made his monastic vows and he became the first disciple of Zosima and Herman. Many coastal inhabitants followed Mark's example. They moved to the isle and, having built their cells near the cells of Zosima and Herman, grew crops and caught fish with nets. Prompted by the fast growing number of disciples, Zosima built a small wooden church in the name of the Transfiguration of the Lord on the place where he received the prophetic vision of the church in the air. He built a small refectory next to it, and so the Solovetski monastery came into being. It still exists nowadays, being protected by God's mercy.

Then Zosima sent one of the monks to Archbishop Jonas in Novgorod, with a request to appoint the hegumen for the monastery and to consecrate the church.

The archbishop appointed as the Solovetski Superior a hieromonk called Paul. Hegumen Paul came to Solovki and consecrated the church in the name of the Transfiguration of the Lord. But he could not stand the hardships of the ascetic life in such a deserted place and soon he returned to Novgorod. The same happened with his successor, hegumen Theodose. Then the brethren of the Solovetski monastery decided during a general meeting that they would not accept superiors coming from other monasteries, but that they would elect a superior amongst themselves. After the election they sent some envoys to the archbishop of Novgorod with the request that he would summon their holy father, Zosima, and would consecrate him as priest and Superior. They asked the archbishop not to pay attention to the unwillingness of the humble Zosima to take this position. The archbishop consented to this request and having summoned Zosima by letter, he convinced him to accept the priesthood and the rank of Father Superior. Zosima received for his monastery rich donations from the citizens, consisting of money, cloths, church utensils and food, and was honourably taken leave of by the archbishop. On his return to Solovki, the brethren joyfully greeted their beloved and respected hegumen. The signs of Gods blessing had increased even more their common respect for the Father Superior. When he celebrated his first liturgy in his monastery, his face shone like that of an angel and the church was filled with an extraordinary fragrance. After the service Zosima blessed some merchants with a prosfora, which they lost, being incautious. The monk, called Macarios, saw outside the church a dog trying to bite something but not succeeding because of the flames that were coming from it. Macarios came nearer and he saw that it was the prosfora that was lost by the merchants. He took it and brought it back the Superior and told him what he had seen, which caused great astonishment among the monks who listened to his story.

As the number of the monks grew, the old wooden church became too small. Zosima had another church built, of a bigger size, in the name of the Dormition of the Mother of God. He also built many monks' cells and so his monastery grew. In addition, he decided for the sake of attracting God's blessing upon his monastery even more, to transfer the relics of Saint Sabbatios to the monastery. Saint Sabbatios had passed away at the mouth of the river Vyga and his relics were buried under the chapel there. He was confirmed in his resolve by a message from the monks of the Cyrillo-Beloyezerski Monastery. 'We heard,' the monks wrote, 'from people from your area, about the Solovetski Isle; that from earliest times it was uninhabited because of the difficulties of sailing to it. And now, they tell us, that by your efforts, according to God's will and owing to the entreaty of the Most Holy Mother of God, a monastery to the glorious Transfiguration of our Lord God and Saviour Jesus Christ has been built. They also tell us that many brethren have gathered together there and that everything is arranged perfectly. You are deprived of just one blessing, namely: you have forgotten Saint Sabbatios, who lived in that place before you, and who passed away in fasting and working. Similar to the ancient holy fathers he was perfect in his virtues. He came to love Christ with his entire soul; he withdrew from the world and received a blissful death. Some of the monks of our monastery, while they were in Novgorod, heard a story of a pious merchant John. He said that on the river Vyga he had the honour to meet Saint Sabbatios and to receive spiritual instructions from him. When Sabbatios had passed away, John, together with hegumen Nathanael, buried him. He also told how God, due to Sabbatios' prayers, has saved him and his brother Theodore from being drowned at sea. We have heard that there were other miracles and wondrous signs which happened in the place where Sabbatios' coffin lies. He is God's servant and we are the witnesses of his virtuous life, as this blessed father lived quite some time together with us in the Cyrillovski monastery. Therefore we give you a spiritual advice: do not deprive yourselves of such a gift and take to your monastery the relics of Saint and Blessed Sabbatios, so that his relics may rest there where he toiled for many years."

  This message was in perfect accordance with the wish of Father Zosima and the Solovetski brethren. They prepared their boat and set out with fair wind to the continent. When they reached the river Vyga and dug out the coffin of Saint Sabbatios, they found his relics and his clothes untouched by decay, spreading an extraordinary fragrance. Singing sacred hymns, the Solovetski monks took the holy relics onto the boat and sailed back to their monastery. At first the glorious relics were laid in the ground, behind the altar of the cathedral of the Dormition. Later they built a chapel above the relics. Many sick people, who came there with faith in their hearts, were healed due to the prayers of Saint Sabbatios. Father Zosima himself prayed ardently in this chapel every night, often until dawn. The merchant John, who was present with his brother Theodore at the burial of Saint Sabbatios, and who had a deep affection for the Saint, painted a portrait of him and presented it together with a generous donation to Father Zosima. Father Zosima accepted the portrait with reverence and having placed it in the chapel of the relics, addressed him with the following words: 'Though the temporary life of your body has ended, we plead to you, stay with us in your spirit, guide us towards God Christ, teaching us to follow the Lord's commandments, to carry our cross and follow our Lord. Having audacity of prayers to Christ and the Most Pure Mother of God, pray and plead for all of us, unworthy ones, who live in this monastery, where you are the head. Be the helper and protector before God of our brotherhood, so that your prayers will protect us from the harm of evil spirits and people and we may glorify the Holy Trinity, the Father, the Son and the Holy Spirit.'

The settling of the monks on the deserted island, the establishment and growth of the Solovetski monastery had awoken envy in the mercenary-minded and malevolent people nearby. Many Korels[6], members of the gentry and their servants, and civil servants had been visiting the island to catch fish in its lakes. However they would not allow the monastery to catch fish, as they considered themselves the owners and the masters of the Solovetski Isle. In the heat of arguments they had

6 A primitive tribe which populated the White Sea coast.

insulted Father Zosima and his monks by abusive words and had been causing trouble for the monastery. They even threatened to destroy the monastery and to drive away all the monks. Father Zosima turned to Theofilos, the archbishop of Novgorod, for help and support. The archbishop received him benevolently and advised Father Zosima to tell those who governed the city, about his needs. Father Zosima visited all of them and asked them to prevent the destruction of the monastery. Almost all the notables promised their help, except Martha Boretzkaya, who was distinguished amongst the members of the Novgorodian gentry for her wealth and influence. It was mostly her serfs and peasants who caused trouble for the monastery. She was biased against Father Zosima because of the slander of her people and when he came to see her, she ordered to throw him disgracefully out of her house. Father Zosima endured this humiliation patiently and meekly. He prophesied to his disciples that the time would come, when the inhabitants of this house would no longer walk in its yard; the doors of the house would be closed and they would never more open and the house would become empty.'

Having noticed that the gentry of the city were in general favourably disposed towards the Solovetski monastery, the archbishop invited them and told them again about the offences that the inhabitants of the coast had been causing the monastery and convinced them to help the monastery. The hegumen received from the benevolent notables many gifts to help the various needs of the monastery: church utensils, garments, gold, silver and bread. Soon after, Martha Boretzkaya repented of her offence towards Father Zosima. Wishing to make amends for her offence she invited him to dinner. Father Zosima, being a forgiving person, accepted her invitation. He was honourably received by her and all her family and he was given a place of honour at the table. All present had been eating and drinking with great pleasure, while Father Zosima was silent and had been eating very little according to his custom. Once when he looked at the other guests, he quickly looked down in amazement; when he looked at them for the second and for the third time he still saw the same: the six most prominent members of the gentry had no head on their shoulders. Having realized the meaning of this vision, Father Zosima sighed and shed some tears. After this he could not eat anything at all, no matter how much his hosts tried to persuade him. After dinner Martha asked Father Zosima forgiveness for her former offence and granted a piece of land to the monastery, confirming it by deed.

When Father Zosima with his disciple Daniel had left the house, Daniel asked him about the reason of his grief and tears during dinner. Father Zosima explained to him his vision, that these six notables would be beheaded some time in the future and he asked his disciple to keep silent about this. Soon after returning to his monastery, his prophecy about the house of Boretzkaya becoming desolated as well as his vision during dinner became true. The great prince Ivan the Third subdued Novgorod by arms and he ordered to put to death the six notables whom Father Zosima saw decapitated. Martha Boretzkaya was sentenced to banishment. Her estate was plundered and it became desolate.

Having reached a venerable age, and having a premonition of his nearing death, Father Zosima began to prepare himself for the passing into eternity. He made a coffin for himself and he looked at it often with tears in his eyes, thinking about his death. When he became ill, he gathered all the brethren and he told them: 'Soon I will leave this temporary life behind, and I will commit you to the All-merciful God and the Most Pure Mother of God: tell me whom you wish to have as my successor.' Then the general love of the disciples for their teacher became obvious. With tears in their eyes the monks told their dying Father Superior: 'Our father, we would like to be buried together with you, but this is beyond our power. Let the One, Who has proclaimed to you your parting from this life, our God Christ, give us through you a mentor who will guide us to our salvation. Let your blessing and your prayers rest upon us. You cared for us in this life, so, do not leave us orphans after you go to God.' Father Zosima answered: 'I told you, children, that I commit you into the hands of the Lord and of the Most Pure Mother of God. However, as regards the new Superior you placed your hope in God, in the Most Pure Mother of God and in my humility, let then Arsenios be your hegumen. He is capable of governing the monastery and the brethren.' Saying this, Father Zosima entrusted the monastery to the pious monk Arsenios. 'Thus I appoint you, brother, as the head of this house and of all the brethren, who have gathered here because of their love for God. Preserve the entire monastery rule unchanged, that is in regard to general church service, meals in the refectory and all other regulations of life in the monastery that I have established. Keep it all unchanged. Let the Lord lead your steps in the fulfilment of His commandments, through the prayers of our Most Pure Lady Virgin and Mother of God and of all the Saints, especially of His servant Saint Sabbatios. Let our Lord Jesus Christ protect you from all the enemy's slander and confirm you in the divine love. I myself, though parting from you bodily, due to our nature, in my spirit, I will remain with you forever. You will come to know whether I have received God's grace when after my death this dwelling will grow and many brethren will live here. This monastery will flourish spiritually and bodily needs will also be taken care of.'

Having said this, he gave the brethren the last kiss, gave them his blessing, prayed for the monastery, for his spiritual flock and for himself with his hands lifted up. Then he crossed himself and said 'Peace be with you!' After looking upwards with eyes which started to grow lifeless he said: 'O merciful Lord, let me stand on Your right side, when You will come in Your Glory to judge the living and the dead and to reward everyone according to their deeds.' Then Father Zosima laid down on his bed and committed his soul to our Lord, for whom he had toiled his entire life. This took place on the 17th April 1478. After the burial service the monks buried the body of their Father Superior in the coffin that he had made himself, behind the altar of the Cathedral of the Transfiguration. After some time they built a chapel above his grave, where they placed holy icons. All the faithful, who visited this place and prayed there received relief of their grief and cure of their diseases. The Moscow assembly which took place in the days of Metropolitan Macarios in 1547 decided to celebrate the memory of Saint Zosima on the 17th April, the day of his passing away. On the 8th August his relics, together with the relics of Saint Sabbatios were placed in the church named after these Miracle-workers, attached to the cathedral. Nowadays the relics of Saint Zosima lie there in a richly decorated shrine.

The Venerable Herman, Solovetski Miracle-Worker

Origin. Simplicity and piety. Visit to the Solovetski Isle. Life at the mouth of the river Vyga near a chapel. Meeting with the ascetic Sabbatios. Life on the Solovetski Isle together with Sabbatios and Zosima. Work for the Monastery. Death. Translation of the holy relics to the Monastery. Appearances of the Saint.

    The Venerable Herman came from the town of Totma. His parents were simple and pious people which was the reason why Herman was not educated and all his life he remained analphabetic. However his mind and heart were cultivated according to the strict rules of Christian ethics and piety. From his youth he aspired to serve God for his salvation. When he came of age he dedicated himself totally to the service of God as a monk. Rumours of the extraordinary suitability of the Solovetski Isle for a solitary ascetic life drew him to the White Sea coast. It was probably in the summer of 1428 that he visited the place of his future ascetic feats together with fishermen. Though the Solvetski Isle corresponded to the wishes of his soul and seemed to him perfectly suitable for practicing complete silence, he nevertheless did not dare to live there alone. When the summer was over, Herman returned with the fishermen to the coast. He settled at the mouth of the river Vyga near a chapel, and lived there, in prayer and fasting.

    But having come to know the Solovetski Isle and feeling love for that place, Herman became the guide and the companion of its first inhabitants: the ascetics Zosima and Sabbatios. Since 1436 Herman had become together with Zosima the permanent resident of this isle, a participant in the prayer practices of Zosima and his zealous assistant in establishing the monastery. Though not learned, Herman was nevertheless convinced that the life of the great ascetics is very edifying. Therefore he asked some monks to note his stories about various events in the lives of the blissful fathers Sabbatios and Zosima on the island. There were many of these notes and one of the disciples of the venerated Herman, called Dositheos, made use of them when he wrote the hagiographies of Saints Zosima and Sabbatios.

Herman lived more than 50 years on the cold island, endeavouring to be as useful as possible for the Monastery. He travelled regularly to the continent during the life of Saint Zosima and also after his death, to care for the different needs of the Monastery. His holy love considered neither the dangers of sailing on the treacherous sea nor other inconveniences of travelling, especially difficult at his great old age. Even death came to him when he was on a journey for some monastery affair. It was in the time of hegumen Arsenios, the successor of Saint Zosima. Herman was sent to Novgorod and in the monastery of Saint Anthony the Roman he felt that his end was near. He confessed and received Holy Communion and then he gave his spirit peacefully to God. His disciples took his body back to the Solovetski Monastery, but as the roads were impassable they buried the coffin near the chapel of the village of Khavronyino on the banks of the river Svir. Five years later, in the days of hegumen Isaiah, the brethren decided to bring the coffin of the venerable Herman to the Solovetski Monastery. The monk sent dug up the coffin and found his relics not touched by decay. The coffin was received in the Monastery very respectfully and it was placed first near the altar, on the right side of the church of Saint Nicolas, near the relics of Saint Sabbatios. Later a chapel was built over his coffin, and in 1860 a stone church was built there in his name.

    The legend tells of an appearance of Saint Herman to a priest called Gregory in the place which is called Old Totma. This was the reason why this priest wrote a troparion in honour of Saint Herman and painted an icon, where Saint Herman was depicted together with Saint Zosima and Saint Sabbatios. The seriously ill pray to this icon and are healed. The celebration of the memory of Saint Herman takes place yearly since 1692 in the Solovetski Monastery on the 30th July with the blessing of Joachim, Patriarch of Moscow and all Russia.

The Venerable Elisha of Soumy

Life. The Scarcity of Information. Illness. Schema. Temptation. Storm. Arrival in Soumy. Death. The Witnessing of the Coffin. The grave of the Venerable one

The Venerable Elisha lived and worked in the Solovetski Monastery at the close of Saint Zosima's life. It could be that he was a co-practitioner of Saint Zosima as the story about the miraculous help of Saint Zosima to Elisha was told by hegumen Bassian, who was hegumen not more than 40 years after the death of Saint Zosima and who in his turn had heard the story about the miracle of Saint Zosima from a very old Starets, who was the co-worker of Elisha in their work of obedience. There is just one feat of Elisha known, where the great piety of this elder was clearly seen and the help from above, which came to him due to the protection of Saint Zosima.

The four brothers: Elisha, Daniel, Philaret and Sabbatios, were doing their work of obedience with the blessing of the hegumen, catching fish in the river Vyga near the rapid Zolotze 63 km away from the Monastery. One day, when they all had been repairing nets, Daniel told Elisha, either due to God's revelation or due to his observations, the following: 'Your work of repairing these nets is in vain as you will not be able to catch fish. Your death is drawing near and your fishing has come to an end.' Terror and fear seized Elisha when he heard this and he started to grieve, but not because he was afraid to die, but because he had not yet taken the great angelic vow, which is the schema. In the neighbourhood there was no hieromonk of sufficient rank who could admit Elisha to this vow[7].

The venerable Elisha of Soumy

The starets became so depressed that even his bodily strength became utterly exhausted. His kind hearted brothers consoled him, convincing him to

7 The sadness and the anxiety of the starets at not being admitted to the great angelic vow are understandable. Even nowadays the monks of Athos all make the great angelic vow; in former times it was done also in our monasteries. The reason of it lies in the teaching of the Church Fathers

entrust himself to God's will, Who sees everything with His omniscient eye, Who sees all the needs of His creatures and Who can fulfil any of their wishes if they call Him from the depth of their soul and with a pure heart. Having noticed however his growing grief and beginning illness, they suggested to him to stand before the invisible presence of God, to pronounce 'Worthy it is and meet...' and having crossed himself, to put on the schema himself and to pray to Saints Zosima and Sabbatios asking for their prayers and blessing. The sick brother accepted this advice and acted accordingly. The night came and the sick brother was put to bed; his tired companions laid down to sleep near him. But when they woke up after a short sleep, the sick brother was absent. They started to search for him and found him without a schema, coming out of the forest. He told them: 'Many devils came to our cell, they attacked me furiously and by force made me go after them. They took the schema from me, but then Saint Zosima saved me and took me away from them.' They found the schema hanging high on a tree. The monks decided to take Elisha to Soumy at any cost, as there was a hieromonk, a permanent resident at the Monastery's coaching inn. They put him in the boat and sailed down the river Vyga. Vyga is a very dangerous river because of the fast stream and a multitude of underwater rapids. The monks often were in commotion because of the dangers, but their sick brother encouraged them saying: 'Don't be afraid, our father Zosima is here with us.' Unharmed they reached the sea and they put in at the mouth of the river Vyrma. The sick one was becoming still more exhausted from disease and he continued grieving of his being deprived of the schema. Another night came. The monks took another boat and hired several oarsmen to speed up the sailing. When they were in the middle of the bay of Soumy, an enormous storm broke out. The waves were towering above the boat; the sail was torn to pieces, the mast was broken and the waves hit the oars from the hands of the rowers. All of them despaired, the oarsmen were grumbling and reproaching the monks, but the sick one did not lose his spirits as he was comforted by a wonderful vision from another world. 'Do not be afraid and do not grieve, brethren', he told his co-farers, hardly being able to breathe because of exhaustion. 'I see our Father Zosima sailing with us on our boat and he is helping us. The storm happened because of the actions of the devil, who wants to destroy my soul, but God will chase the enemy away, because of the prayers of the venerated Zosima.' Soon after, the wind subsided little by little and the waves calmed down and the sailors suddenly found themselves near the landing-stage of Soumy which they could not even hope to find as the boat was deprived of the sail and the oars and was driven, deep in the night, just by the waves. Having put in there, the monks discovered with terror that the sick one was dead and their joy turned immediately into grief. Weeping bitterly they called onto Zosima: 'Oh our venerated father, relying on your prayers we endured such toiling, such dangers on the sea, and it was all in vain and we did not receive what we hoped to receive. However, after a while, they noticed some movement from the body of the deceased, then his mouth opened and he started to speak sensibly. He was brought to the coaching inn, he was admitted to the great angelic vow and received the Divine Sacraments, the Body and the Blood of Christ. Elisha thanked God and having bode farewell to all present, he passed again to his rest in the Lord. His body was buried behind the altar of the Saint Nicolas Church, on the southern side. Years passed and many had even forgotten his name. More than a hundred years later, he was remembered when suddenly his coffin came to the surface. Soon after the appearance of the Venerated one the healing of the sick started through him. In order to verify the reality of the events, in 1668 the Tsar's retainer, called Alexander Sebastianovitch Khitorvo was sent to Soumy. After the investigation Khitorvo erected a small chapel above the coffin of the venerated Elisha. The second examination about the venerated Elisha took place in 1710 upon the decree of Raphael, the archbishop of Kholmogory, at the time of the Solovetzki hegumen archimandrite Thyrsos.

Nowadays the grave of the venerated Elisha is situated under the altar of a new wooden church, and a new wooden shrine with a portrait of the Venerated one on it. Services are held there for the venerable Elisha, but also the office for the dead, when the church visitors wish to commemorate their dead relatives, who had the same name as him. The inhabitants of Soumy consider it as their duty to visit his chapel after each Liturgy and to honour his memory. Also, they pray to him for his blessing before they set out to fish. His appearances and healing of the sick take place also nowadays for those who pray with faith for his help. The celebration of the memory of the venerable Elisha takes place locally on the 14th July.

Blessed Theodoretos, missionary to the Lopars

Origin. Education. Monastic vows. Hierodeacon. Visits to different Monasteries. Home-coming. Preaching to the Lopars. Hieromonk. Hegumen. Archimandrite. Imprisonment. Visit to Constantinople. Death

A native of Rostov, Theodoretos left his parents and came to the Solovetski monastery. In a year's time, at the age of 14, he made his monastic vows and was entrusted as a novice to an old and rather wise hieromonk, Zosima[8]. Theodoretos served in the Monastery for fifteen years without leaving it. Having become spiritually wise he firmly practiced all virtues, and the archbishop of Novgorod consecrated him hierodeacon. Theodoretos lived one more year with his elder and then asked his permission to travel in order to visit other monasteries. First of all he went to the venerated Alexander Svirsky, who received him kindly and on their meeting called him by his first name. He visited some other monasteries and settled in the Cyrillo-Byeloyezerski Monastery, where he met elder Serge and other holy men. He remained in this monastery for two years and then he visited the hermitages around the Cyrillovsky monastery. There, he met Porfirios, who in 1521-1534 was Father Superior of the Sergiev Monastery, Artemios, Joasaf and other hermits with a high standard of ascetic life, who were already very old. Theodoretos had spent

[8] It was probably that very Zosima, who is mentioned in the hagiography of the Solovetski Founders. In 1485 he lived near the river Shouya and Saints Zosima and Sabbatios gave, through him, their support to the Monastery which was burned down.

about four years with them when he received a letter from his Solovetski elder. His teacher had a presentiment of his nearing death and he asked his disciple to come to him. Neither the great distance, nor the difficulties of the journey could withhold Theodoretos. He rushed to his teacher in order to embrace the aged elder and to kiss his holy head with veneration. Theodoretos served his elder who was feeble and ill, for about a year, until his blissful death.

After this Theodoretos resolved to undertake a feat on the scale of the Apostles and to go to the mouth of the river Kola, where the tribe of wild Lopars lived. He learned their language in the Solovetski Monastery. This was possible because, as the Life of Saints Zosima and Sabbatios tells us, many members of the wild tribes neighbouring the Monastery, like the Izhora, Tchoud, Lopye, Kayans and Mourmans had been coming to the Monastery asking for holy Baptism and becoming monks.

Lopars were utterly savage idol worshipers, they bowed before idols, deified bats, reptiles and vermin; they ate impure and filthy food; they did not know how to live in cities and settlements but lived as isolated families. However they had simple hearts, and the seeds of God's word put there could bring forth good fruit. Theodoretos translated some Orthodox prayers into the Lopar language and taught them the basics of faith. His assistant in the conversion of Lopars to Christianity was elder Metrofan. Theodoretos worked twenty years for this sacred cause. After that he was ordained a hieromonk in Novgorod and was for some time the confessor of the Metropolitan. Later he returned to the Lopars and founded a monastery there. But soon after he had to leave the monastery because of the hatred of the monks, who did not want to follow his strict rule. By that time he had already baptized two thousand Lopars. He went to the Novgorod region and was Father Superior of one of the monasteries there, till he was summoned to Moscow and was appointed archimandrite of the Spaso-Evfimiev Monastery in Suzdal[9]. There he was hegumen for five years with the rank of archimandrite until 1554, but being calumniated by heretics, who were like-minded persons with Bashkin[10], the hard-working elder was sentenced to two years confinement in the Cyrillo-Byeloyezerski Monastery. After being discharged he lived for some time in the Monastery of Yaroslavl. Tsar Ivan the Terrible summoned him to Moscow and in 1558 the Tsar sent him to Constantinople to talk to the Patriarch on the subject of his coronation. Theodoretos brought the Tsar the Patriarch's answer and for this service the Tsar gave him 300 silver coins and a sable fur coat, covered with brocade. Theodoretos, who did not care about money, accepted 25 silver coins only. As to the fur coat, the monk sold it and gave the money to the poor. Then he retired to the Monastery of Priluki in the Vologodskaya province. Twice he visited the Lopars he had converted, and finally, after his great labour and many difficulties he went to his eternal rest at the place where he had made his monastic vow, the Solovetski Monastery. He was buried near the south wall of the Transfiguration Cathedral. There is still a white plate with the following inscription: 'In the year 7079 (1571), August 17th, God's servant the monk Theodoretos, archimandrite of the Evphimi Monastery of Suzdal, who made his monastic vows in the Solovetski Monastery. The Church gave him, for his ascetic life and educational work the title 'Blessed'.

---

9 A small town not far from Moscow
10 See: https://en.wikipedia.org/wiki/Matvei_Bashkin

The Venerable Hegumen Philip, the future Holy Metropolitan of Moscow and all Russia

Origin. Education. The church service at the court on 5th July 1537. Banishment from Moscow. Residence in Khizhi. Arrival at the Solovetski Monastery. Work of Obedience. Monastic vow. Hermit's life. Hegumen. Improving the Monastery's economy. Buildings. Construction of the Cathedral of the Dormition. Foundations of the Transfiguration Cathedral. Administration of the rural districts. An example of asceticism. Honoured by the tsar. Invitation to Moscow. Departure. Election as Metropolitan. Care for the Solovetski Monastery. Conversation with the tsar. Consoling the grieving. The 21st March and the 28th July in the year 1568. Investigation. The trial on 8th November. The last consolation for the tsar. Imprisonment. Disgrace of the Kolychev family. Martyr's death. The retribution of the slanderers. Translation of the relics to the Solovetski Monastery. Glorification. Translation of the relics to Moscow

    The Solovetski Monastery was the place were the great illuminator of the Russian Church, Metropolitan Philip of Moscow, who was adorned with the martyr's halo, grew up spiritually and made his monastic vows. It was the place where he not only learned spiritual practices but where for many years, being most experienced and skilful, as hegumen, he led other monks on the path of salvation. Therefore the Solovetski Monastery considers him justly as one of its ascetics and especially lovingly praises his name.

This great Churchman came from the celebrated Kolychev family. His father Stephen was a retainer of the Great Prince Basil, son of John, and his mother, named Barbara was distinguished by her piety and love for the poor. On 11th February 1507 their first child was born and was given the name Theodore.

St. Philip, Metropolitan of Moscow and Russia, and martyr

His parents brought him up with great care. When he reached the age of seven they started to teach him to read and write according to the customs of their time, using church books. The youth liked school, especially reading spiritual books and he was already in his early years very pious.

After the death of the Great Prince Basil, during the reign of his wife Helen, Theodore joined the court. He had an excellent position there enjoying the favour of the princess regent and being the retainer of the infant John IV. However Theodore's heart wasn't flattered by fame and outer splendour and was not attached to the world. On the 5th July 1537, which was the third Sunday after Pentecost, he heard during the liturgy the words of the Gospel: 'None can serve two masters; he will either hate the one and will love the other, or he will do his best for the one, and neglect the other.' (Math., 6, 24) Of course Theodore had heard these words more than once before, but this time God's grace touched him. His heart flared up with the fire of love for God. He rejected all that was of this world and he decided to retire to a deserted place and to serve God.

It was Theodore's intention to run far away and for ever from the world and all its temptations. Pondering upon this he remembered the Solovetski Monastery, which was situated on a desolate isle in the cold sea and in this way separated by nature itself from the world. He remembered also the ascetic feats of its founders, Saint Sabbatios, Saint Zosima and Saint Herman, who had brought Christianity to the Northern areas. The innermost thoughts of Theodore aspired for this place. Preparing himself for the long journey, in Moscow he bowed before the relics of the Miracle-workers, praying in stillness: 'Oh Lord God, my Saviour and the Defender of my life! Teach my Thy way so that I may walk in Thy truth.'

When a convenient moment came he exchanged the rich garments of a courtier for the poor clothes of the low classes and he left Moscow. Heading for the North and walking along roads unknown to him Theodore reached Lake Onega. He made a halt in one of the numerous villages on the bank of the lake, called Khizhi, to have a rest, but perhaps also to hide. He was kindly invited to stay by a kind peasant called Sabbatios. The stories about the remoteness of the Solovetski Isle and his lack of means to continue on his way made him accept Sabbatios' hospitality. Theodore however did not want to be a burden to his host and he worked for Sabbatios. Soon Theodore gained his host's trust and was put to work as a shepherd, watching the sheep. Quite some time passed in these rural activities and the appearance of the stranger who had become accustomed gradually to the simple and unfamiliar labour changed. It was difficult to recognize the former courtier in this shepherd. The autumn came, bringing storms and ice, which made all communication with the Solovetski Isle impossible. When spring came Theodore bode his host farewell and left for the so longed for aim of his journey. His parents, who meanwhile had been searching everywhere for him, mourned him as having passed away.

The hegumen of Solovki Father Alexis and the brethren accepted the newcomer with love, not knowing his famous family. He was placed with the novices who worked in the Monastery. Theodore humbly accepted the duties which were laid on him. For more than a year and a half he did this heavy work of obedience without weakening in his zeal. 'It was amazing to see,' his contemporary biographer narrates, 'how this boy, a son of famous and celebrated parents, who had a most comfortable and quiet childhood and youth, was doing hard work, cutting wood, digging in the kitchen-garden, carrying stones, lifting heavy nets for fishing and doing it all zealously. He often had to carry sacks of manure on his back and he also worked diligently at the mill. It happened more than once that he had to endure beatings and humiliation from rough and unreasonable people. Theodore however followed the example of the Lord Christ and endured it humbly, and his true origin and his name remained unknown. At the same time Theodore attentively watched the way of life of the Solovetski monks. He caused their astonishment by his determination in following them and stripping himself of worldly passions. Finally, burning still more with the fire of love for God, he prostrated himself before the hegumen and the brethren asking them to reckon him among their chosen flock. As the hegumen and the brethren themselves saw his great longing and the strength of his will for what was good, they lovingly listened to his request. Theodore was admitted to make his monastic vows and he received the name Philip.

The new monk received as his teacher hieromonk Jonas, who admitted him to the monastic consecration. Jonas led an elevated life and in his youth he was for some time in contact with the venerated Alexander Svirski, who later was recognized as Saint. Philip settled in the cell of the pious elder, learning from him various virtues. He spent his days working and fasting, and his nights praying, often even forgetting to sleep. Jonas was pleased by the zeal of his disciple and he prophesised about him to the brethren: 'This one will become hegumen of our monastery.' Philip was appointed overseer of the monastery's forge where he had to carry out heavy work, and the constant presence of fire reminded him of the fire of hell; then he was sent to the bakery, where he also wasn't idle, but willingly carried water and firewood. At the first stroke of the church bell Philip was there to attend the service. The Lord rewarded the humility of His worker: there is still in the Transfiguration Cathedral an icon of the Mother of God that is called 'The Bakery Icon'; this icon appeared to Philip during his work of obedience in the bakery. It is a kind of proof that it is not the type of work of obedience which matters, but our zeal in carrying it out that brings us closer to God. Finally he was appointed ecclesiarch of the cathedral and in this position he gained general praise, respect and love.

However, Philip was afraid of even the slightest hint of fame and in his humble soul there grew a longing for a life in silent seclusion. He left the monastery and lived in the middle of the island in the thickest of a wild and impenetrable forest. There, mortifying his flesh and gaining full control of his thoughts he gave himself over to prayer and conversing with God. He practised this for many years. When he became experienced and firmly established in silence and inner prayer, he returned to the monastery in order to work with his brethren. The pious hegumen found in him a great support and consolation. He appointed Philip as his assistant in various fields. Philip had become the hegumen's right hand and 'the support of his old age'. With the filial love of an obedient son he cared for his elder when he was ill and consoled him in his grief. In the year 1584 Alexis, feeling that his end was drawing near and being aware of Philip's virtues, started to give him hints that he wished to transmit the task of hegumen to him. Philip however did not even want to hear a word about it. Neither Alexis' admonitions nor the request of the brethren could make him change his mind. The hegumen, inwardly pleased at Philip's humility, wished even more to break down Philip's resistance. He called all the monks together and having told them about his old age and feebleness he asked them who they would wish to have as their hegumen. They all answered as one man that none could be compared to Philip in his way of life, his intelligence and experience in the ascetic practices. Philip could not contradict the general gathering. The hegumen sent him, accompanied by several brethren, and with the application, to Novgorod, to archbishop Theodose, who was already informed about the purpose of their journey. 'Why don't I see him with you?' he asked the envoy when he saw them alone, without Philip. During the meeting with Philip, which came soon after, Theodose saw in him an enlightened and deep intelligence and great spiritual experience. He ordained Philip hieromonk and gave him the hegumen's staff.

The old hegumen Alexis together with all the brethren in procession met Philip solemnly on the landing-stage. Together they went to the cathedral where the old hegumen offered his place to Philip. Having read aloud the edict of the archbishop, the new hegumen preached his first sermon to the brethren and asked the priests and the deacons to prepare themselves for the Divine liturgy. On 17th August 1548 he celebrated his first liturgy with several other priests. However, even then Philip did not dare to take on himself the burden of elder. Having noticed that Alexis' strength was coming back, he convinced the elder to continue being the superior and promised that he would be perfectly obedient to the elder. Though this was against his will, Alexis accepted the staff again, while Philip withdrew once more to his beloved hermitage, and his seclusion was even stricter than before. One and a half year passed before Alexis became completely exhausted and Philip was called back as superior again. Having buried the elder Philip took over the work of elder, upon the request of the monks, and he continued his practices. He was an example of all virtues for the monks, not only in words but also in deeds, excelling all the monks in his inner and outer work.

Philip was hegumen for eighteen years, counting from the day when he was nominated until the day he was summoned to take the place of Metropolitan of all Russia. His time as hegumen left an indelible trace in the monastery; truly, if people would stay silent, the stones would testify to it! In all the spheres of life and activity of the monastery his wise sagacity was noticeable. It bore fruit not only for that time but also for the future well-being of the monastery. A good organizer, a meek ruler, a wise teacher in the field of spiritual activity: these were the main qualities of Saint Philip during his period as hegumen.

At the beginning of his rule, the monastery's economy had difficulties, as the number of monks grew while the resources were poor. In addition to it the monastery had not yet rebuilt its buildings which were burnt in the year 1538. Since old times the main source of income for the monastery was salt. Philip started improving this particular trade and he increased the number of salt-works on the sea-shore to six units. Tsar Ivan the Terrible was favourably disposed towards the monastery and in 1548 he granted the monastery permission to sell tax-free 10.000 pud (160.000 kg) of salt instead of the former 6.000 pud (96.000 kg) and also to purchase tax-free from this income all that the monastery needed.

Having arranged a cattle-yard on the Muxalmski Isle, about 14 km away from the monastery, Philip improved in this way the brethren's meals. He had deer brought in and released in the forests of the isle to make clothes and shoes from the skins.

He decided to build in stone to replace the burnt wooden buildings and for this he established a brick factory. He personally pointed out special places for tree-felling to have firewood for the factory so that the forest would not be damaged, but on the contrary, would be cleared and grow even better. He had roads built through the forests, the mountains and the swamps: human intelligence was adapting the deserted island for human needs. He had a mill built in the monastery. In order to supply the mill with sufficient running water, the hegumen selected amongst numerous lakes the 52 lakes which were situated most conveniently and had the best water. He had a network of channels dug connecting all these lakes, and a huge pond near the monastery which was connected to this system of lakes by a channel. This pond was later named 'The Holy Lake' and supplies the monastery even nowadays with fresh sweet water.

In order to make the entrance to the bay where the monastery is situated, visible for ships, the hegumen ordered to make high mounds on the shore and erect big crosses on them. He had built in the harbour of Zayatzki Isle a stone pier with a big house and a kitchen, and in the monastery two- and three storey buildings with cells for the brethren were built.

Amidst all these concerns St. Philip, without doubting God's mercy, in 1552 started building the Cathedral of the Dormition of the Mother of God, with an attached church dedicated to the Beheading of John the Forerunner with a spacious refectory. Not having enough means to fulfil such enormous projects the hegumen turned first to Tsar Ivan the Terrible who was especially generous for the Solovetski monastery. In 1550 the tsar granted the monastery the Kolezhemski rural district, with its villages, fields and forests, and the salt-works. Next year the tsar granted the monastery the coastal village of Sorotzkaya, where Saint Sabbatios was first buried near the walls of the Trinity church. In order to build the Dormition Cathedral skilful architects where invited from Novgorod. In 1557, on the day of the feast of the Dormition, Philip could joyfully consecrate the cathedral. Having just finished the building of this cathedral the indefatigable hegumen announced to the brethren his intention to build an even more spacious and magnificent cathedral dedicated to the Transfiguration of our Lord. Some of the monks had the courage to express their apprehensions to the hegumen and they told him: 'Father, the monastery's economy has shortages, its treasury is poor, we are far away from the cities: where could we possibly find finances to build such a huge temple!' 'Brethren,' Philip answered, 'hope in God is not in vain: if the Lord is pleased with our cause, He will grant us in an invisible way a part of his inexhaustible treasures, and the house of His holy Name will be most certainly built.' The monks were quiet. 'Let it be as you wish,' they said, 'God will give anything you ask from Him.'

Philip's love of this project was specially strong and everything during the building of the cathedral was done under his vigilant supervision. Sometimes he participated in the manual labour himself, arousing zeal in the workers by his own example. The tsar was again amongst the investors in this cathedral: in 1558 he gave 1000 roubles for the building, and in 1559 he granted the monastery the tax-free transport of the salt and tax-free purchase of different goods for the monastery. Philip however could not witness the end of the construction of the cathedral but he prepared the necessary utensils, coloured glass for the windows, the vessels, the books, the garments, the icons, the precious fabrics, silver candelabras, censers, and dug a grave for himself under the northern end of the church-porch.

Besides improving the life in the monastery Philip had to establish order in the administration of the rural districts. In those times the Solovetski monastery had in its possession some populous rural districts. The monastery was granted the right to be legal authority in the districts with regard to all matters, except the criminal cases. The hegumen's primary concern was to organize an effective district administration, in accordance with the spirit of the time. For this he appointed some of the monastery's elders as manager, treasurer and a kind of judge in each of the districts. Their living was provided by the collection and some casual taxes. Besides this the hegumen issued new rules for the legal proceedings and the collection of taxes.

The time was approaching when hegumen Philip was to leave the Solovetsky monastery and be elevated to the high office of Metropolitan of all Russia. The good fruit resulting from his work appeared not only in the cloister itself. He attended to all the needs of the peasants in the villages belonging to the monastery; the monastery even supplied the villages with wood to make salt. The hegumen himself instructed what work to do and when to do it and even what seeds should be sown in the fields. He forbade the most pernicious vices - hard drinking and the gambling game of dice called zern – under the threat of being driven out of the monastery village.

Hegumen Philip placed great emphasis on the spiritual life of the brethren. "Accomplishing one feat after another, ascending from one virtue to another, he touched the hearts by his own example rather than by words, by the power of love rather than by the power of authority". Four ascetics who joined the monastery when he was hegumen are glorified by the Church : the venerated Bassian and Jonah Pertominsky and the laymen John and Longin Yarengsky.

Ivan the Terrible showed his favour to the monastery by favouring hegumen Philip personally. The Tsar summoned him to Moscow many times. In 1566 he was called upon by a special official document "For the sake of the synod". The hegumen was sixty years old at that time.

On his way to the capital he passed through Novgorod. Knowing about the anger of Ivan the Terrible, the citizens asked him to be their defender. The Tsar informed hegumen Philip that according to his sovereign will and the synod's decision he was chosen as metropolitan. The hegumen asked Ivan the Terrible not to separate him from his Monastery. The Tsar was inexorable and ordered the bishops and boyars to persuade Philip. The hegumen of the Solovetsky Monastery agreed to accept this office on condition that the Oprichnina (the personal guard of Ivan the Terrible, which terrorized Russia) would be abolished.

Philip was received by the court of Ivan the Terrible with hostility. The Tsar did not express his anger directly but in an official document ordered that "the bishops and archbishops should tell Philip to abandon his claim and not to interfere in court affairs and the Oprichnina". Hegumen Philip had to yield to the Tsar's will.

He was ordained Metropolitan of Moscow and All Russia on July 25th 1566 (all dates are according to the Julian Calendar). The Tsar himself seemed moved by the metropolitan's peaceable speech.

Having taken upon himself the burden of this new office, metropolitan Philip "remained united in spirit with his beloved desert". He did not forget the brethren of the Solovetsky Monastery and received them with great joy whenever they came. He built a church dedicated to the Wonderworkers of Solovki and he ordered to complete the construction of the lake on Solovki which had not been finished while he was there.

"St. Philip's soul had a good reason to yearn for the peaceful cloister of Solovki: the clouds were gathering over the metropolitan's head. In January 1567 the Tsar moved from the Kremlin to his fortified palace, where he was surrounded only by the oprichniks (members of the Oprichnina) and was totally in their hands. In a general silence everybody hoped to hear the only salutary voice of Philip".

The metropolitan appealed to the bishops, but "there was no unanimity amongst them". It did not frighten him and he decided to accomplish a feat without any helpers. First not publicly and then in public he began to condemn the Tsar. "Your Majesty the Tsar!" the prelate said courageously, "Discern the sly from the truthful; accept good advisers, not flatterers. It is sinful not to prevent sinners, but you should not divide the unity of the realm! You are appointed by God to judge His people fairly, but you are not to torture them. Unmask those who do not tell you the truth…"

After such meetings the Tsar would be gloomy and pensive. Maluta Skuratov and Basil Gryaznoy were good at using this mood and roused Ivan's anger about these just words.

Metropolitan Philip consoled and encouraged the sorrowful. "The axe is close to the root, but do not be frightened and remember that God promises us not earthly but heavenly blessings. I am happy that I can suffer for you: I am responsible for you to God, you are my God-given crown".

On the Sunday of the Veneration of the Cross, March 21st 1569, when the metropolitan was standing at the bishop's place in the Dormition

Cathedral, Ivan with the oprichniks wearing black cassocks over their caftans and high black hats entered the church. The Tsar bowed his head three times wishing to receive the metropolitan's blessing but Philip kept on looking at the icon. The tsar's followers said: "Holy Lord! The Tsar of all Russia, Ivan Vasilyevich, demands your blessing. "

The metropolitan addressed the Tsar with a condemning speech: "How long shall the Orthodox believers suffer?! Tatars and heathens have law and justice but we do not have them; one can find mercy everywhere but there is no compassion for the innocent in Russia."

Ivan whispered threats, knocked with his staff on the rostrum and said, while making threatening gestures: "How dare you, Philip, oppose our power! Let us see how great your fortitude is."

The metropolitan was doomed to death, but Ivan did not hurry to kill him. Slanderers were allowed to act. The Tsar himself avoided meeting the metropolitan. The prelate moved from the Kremlin to the Nikolsky Monastery situated in Nikolskaya street. On July 28th an incident occurred which gave Ivan the Terrible cause to start an investigation. Philip was celebrating a service at the Novodevichy Monastery with a procession outside in the Tsar's presence. When the procession reached the holy gate, before reading the Gospel the metropolitan turned to the people to say "peace to all", but he saw one of the oprichniks wearing a tatar tafia(a kind of hat). The prelate asked the Tsar to look at the boyar who was blaspheming, but when the Tsar turned to him the boyar had already bared his head. Then Ivan called the metropolitan a deceiver and a rebel. The boyars of the metropolitan's court were taken into custody and tortured.

Torturing the boyars did not give any results and there was nothing to accuse the prelate of. Then bishop Paphnutios who treated the Metropolitan with malevolence, archimandrite Theodosios, prince Basil Temkin, deacon Pivov accompanied by a military escort were ordered to go to Solovki. First they distributed money and then resorted to threats trying to persuade the monks of Solovki to give false evidence. Finally Paphnutios enticed hegumen Paissios and he in his turn enticed some monks and they went all together to Moscow to slander the saint.

Ivan the Terrible ordered the boyars and bishops to gather in the Dormition Cathedral to subject the metropolitan to an open trial. After the denunciations had been read, metropolitan Philip, not considering it necessary to justify himself, addressed the Tsar with the following words: "Tsar! You are wrong if you think that I am afraid either of you or of death. I have been a hermit since my youth and I have preserved my honor and chastity... when I die, I wish people to remember me as an innocent martyr instead of as a man who may be said to have suffered injustice and dishonor being metropolitan".

The prelate began to take off the attributes of his office, but the Tsar stopped him saying that he should wait for the decision of the council and asked him to celebrate the Liturgy in the Dormition Cathedral three days later, on November 8th. During the service Alexis Basmanov and the oprichniks entered the church, interrupted the divine service and began to read a bill of accusations. The oprichniks attacked the prelate and began to tear his vestments off.

The prelate was forced to put on a ragged monk's habit, was then beaten with brooms, put on a woodsledge and taken out of the Kremlin. The people seeing the metropolitan being abused blocked Nikolskaya Street. Philip said: "Children! I have done everything I could; if it were not for my love for you,

I would not have stayed here a single day; trust in God!"

The righteous was taken into custody and imprisoned in the Theophany Monastery. The next day he was taken with much abuse to the metropolitan's palace where he met the Tsar with the bishops and the oprichniks. There, he also met his successor in the Solovetsky Monastery, hegumen Paissios who had slandered him. Metropolitan Philip condemned the Tsar publicly for the last time.

By order of the Tsar the saint was put in a dungeon. He was shackled and a stack of straw served him as a bed. He was 62 at that time.

They did not give food to the prisoner hoping to starve him to death. When the messengers of the Tsar came to him, they saw him praying, free from his shackles. When Ivan the Terrible heard about it, he exclaimed: "Sorcery!" He forbade the incident being divulged and ordered to lock up a hungry bear with the prisoner. In the morning the Tsar went himself to see and saw the saint praying and the bear lying quietly in the corner.

The Tsar decided to imprison the metropolitan in the Monastery of St. Nicholas the Old. The sum of four altyns (an old Russian currency with a value of three kopecks) a day was allotted to maintain him. The whole Kolychev family was subjected to torture and execution. About ten relatives of the metropolitan died one after another in torture chambers. They brought the prelate the head of his nephew, the son of his younger brother, Commander Boris. The Tsar ordered to present it to him with the following words: "Here is your relative's head: your sorcery did not help him".

"The prelate accepted the cruel gift with awe, put the bloodstained head in front of him, made a low bow before it, kissed it with tears and said: "They are blessed, for You have chosen and accepted them,

O Lord, may their memory live from generation to generation", and gave it back to the messenger.

People were constantly gathering near the Nikolsky cloister. Ivan ordered to transfer the prisoner from Moscow to the Otroch Monastery (Monastery of the Fathers) of Tver. On the way the saint endured every humiliation, cold and hunger.

In December 1569 Ivan the Terrible headed with his band of warriors for Novgorod. His route passed through Tver. Before reaching the town, the Tsar sent Maluta Skuratov to the prelate as if to receive his blessing.

Maluta entered the cell, bowed humbly and said: "Holy Lord, give your blessing to the Tsar to go to Novgorod". Saint Philip knew the reason for Maluta's coming and without losing his usual serenity he said: "Do what you must and do not blaspheme". Then the saint turned to the icon and began to pray. The oprichnik grabbed a pillow, put it on the saint's mouth and suffocated him. Then Skuratov ran out of the cell and began to reproach the wardens and the superior, saying that the metropolitan had died because of the excessive heat in the cell. Everybody was horrified. Maluta ordered to dig a deep grave behind the altar of the cathedral and to put the body there in his presence. It happened on December 23rd 1569.

In 1591 during the reign of Tsar Theodore Ivanovich the relics of metropolitan Philip were transferred to the Solovetsky Monastery where they were put in the grave that had been chosen by the prelate himself and there they remained for fifty five years.

"Since the translation of the relics of Metropolitan Philip to Solovki, the northern lands of Russia prayed to him for his intercession. In May 1636 the service was compiled which has since then been used to glorify the saint. In 1646 during the reign of

Tsar Alexis Mikhailovich it was decided to expose the relics, and in the beginning of 1652 the decision was taken to transfer them to the Dormition Cathedral in Moscow".

The memory of Saint Philip is celebrated on the following days:

January 9/22 – Celebration of the memory of Philip, Metropolitan of Moscow and all Russia, Wonder-worker (1569);

May 31 / June 13 – Translation of the relics of Philip, Metropolitan of Moscow, from the interior of the Earth to the Church of the Transfiguration of the Lord (1646);

July 3 / 16 - Translation of the relics of Philip, Metropolitan of Moscow and all Russia, Wonder-worker (1652);

August 9 /22 – Celebration of the Synaxis of the Saints of Solovki.

The Venerable John and Longin of Yarenga (+1561)

The venerable John and Longin worked in the Solovetsky Monastery under the guidance of the hegumen St Philip, leading a life of strict fasting and prayer. Their constant rule was the word of the Apostle: "Whatsoever ye do, do it heartily, as to the Lord, and not unto men" (Colossians 3:23). Though they were not educated, they were brought up in the fundamentals of Christianity and their simple mind and pure heart drew important lessons by contemplating the greatness of nature. They would see the vast sea and think about the Creator who had put boundaries to the sea; the starry sky would turn their eyes to God, who had established a strict order for everything. Thus in the silence of the cloister these simple people climbed from one level of perfection to another until the Lord wished to call them to the ineffable Light.

In 1561, while sailing back to the cloister on ships loaded with construction material, they were caught by a violent storm and drowned. Their holy bodies were found incorrupt on the shore of Karelia, 120 km from the monastery of Solovki, and buried in the village of Yarenga.

Soon the fame of the miracles happening near the saints' relics attracted several ascetics. They built cells nearby, thus founding a monastery in Yarenga.

In 1622 the monastery, situated next to the village along the seashore, included a wooden church of St. Nicholas the Wonder-worker, cells, a refectory and a chapel. Starets Barlaam, Triphon and Ermolaus Teloves were in charge of the church and it was well furnished with icons, books, candles and bells. Services were celebrated by hieromonk Matthew.

The venerable John and Longin of Yarenga

In 1625 the ascetic Elias Telov told patriarch Philaret about the miracles happening near the saints' relics. As a consequence the metropolitan of Novgorod, Macarios, ordered hegumen Gerasimos of the Nikolsky Monastery of Karelia, together with Solonov, the son of a boyar of the metropolitan's house, to conduct a thorough inquiry about the date of the finding of the relics and the miracles performed by the venerated John and Longin. The information in the report made by the ascetic Elias proved to be true, and besides, it turned out that miracles had been taking place for sixty years. The most remarkable healings at that time were the following: the healing of Maria, who for three years had been possessed; the healing of a young villager who had suffered from epilepsy, and of the villager Euphemios who had suffered from stomach aches and who was called to Yarenga by the apparition of the venerated John and Longin.

In 1635 following the petition of Patriarch Joasaph and the official document issued by Tsar Michael Fyodorovich the Yarengsky Monastery with all its lands and the village of Yarenga fell within the jurisdiction of the Solovetsky Monastery. Metropolitan Aphon of Novgorod informed archimandrite Raphael, who was the head of the Solovetsky Monastery, about this and ordered him to build a new church and to consecrate it in honour of the Wonder-workers of Solovki Zosima and Sabbatios, for "the Wonder-workers of Yarenga, John and Longin, worked in the Solovetsky Monastery". "I would like you to write to me as soon as the church is built", added the Metropolitan, "and the relics of the newly recognized Wonder-workers John and Longin are transferred to the new church and the place for them is chosen".

A new wooden church was built and consecrated by hegumen Bartholomew, the successor of archimandrite Raphael who was transferred in 1636 to the Khutynsky Monastery of Novgorod. On July 2nd 1638, the relics of the saints were transferred to this church; John's relics were put on the right side and Longin's relics on the left side. The Yarengsky Monastery remained in the jurisdiction of the Solovetsky Monastery until it was closed in 1764 when the "Ecclesiastical classification" was introduced. According to the "Solovetsky Patericon" (Moscow, 1906) the holy relics of the venerated John and Longin rest in the parish church of Yarenga.

The memory of the Venerable John and Longin is celebrated on July 3/16 and on August 9/22.

The Venerable Bassian and Jonah of Pertominsk (+1561)

The venerable Bassian and Jonah were contemporaries of St Philip, hegumen and later metropolitan of Moscow and all Russia, and they were instructed in their spiritual and ascetic life under his guidance. As hegumen Philip emphasized the spirit of diligence and obedience and tried to maintain it in the monks, being himself an example of all virtues.

When the hegumen was building stone churches in the monastery he needed various construction materials which were brought to the seashore on monastery ships. In 1561 when fifteen ships were sailing to the monastery from the mouth of the river Dvina, there was a sudden violent storm and all the ships were wrecked. Many of the people who were on these ships drowned including the venerated Bassian and Jonah.

The waves cast the ascetics' bodies on the eastern side of the Ounskaya Bay. The villagers who were sailing to fish in the Ounskya Bay approached the place where the bodies of the venerated ones were lying and saw many ravens flying over them as if being frightened away by some invisible force. The bodies were unharmed and incorrupt. The fishermen wanted to take them to their village and bury them with honour near the parish church. But after they had put the bodies in their boat and were sailing to their village, mist and darkness suddenly surrounded them and they lost their way; as a result they came again to the place where the bodies had been found. They had a vision in which the venerable Bassian and Jonah appeared and said: "Put us in an open space in the pine forest under a big pine but do not take us to your village; having taken us from the water you do not want to put us to the water again. If God wishes He will build a church in this place". Then the fishermen remembered that their village is really situated in a damp location and obeying the venerated monks' wish they buried their bodies in the pine forest under a pine and put a wooden cross over the grave.

The Venerable Bassian and Jonah of Pertominsk

In 1599 Mamant, starets of the Troitse-Serguiev Monastery, came to the Unskaya Bay and was delayed there by a strong wind for four days. While asleep he saw in a dream two men, and when he asked them: "Where are you from? What are your names?" one of them said his name was Bassian, and the other said his name was Jonah; then they told him how they had drowned, showed the place of their burial and asked him to build a chapel over the grave. On June12th the starets built a chapel over the relics of the venerated monks and put a cross on it. Then a favourable wind blew and he continued his journey.

The miracles and apparitions of the venerable monks made the place of their burial famous throughout the northern land, so travellers and seamen landing on the shore considered it their duty to pray in the chapel and to leave offerings of money and candles there.

Once an elder came to the village by the Ounskaya Bay. The villagers told him about the venerable Bassian and Jonah and advised him to settle near the chapel. The elder followed their advice and having prayed to God, built a small cell near the chapel. Soon afterwards starets Sabbatios and Dionisios settled near him and later again hieromonk Ephrem and the layman Cosmas and his son joined them. The hermits decided to build a church over the relics and began to cut trees. A sudden incident helped them very much: two boats sailing to the Solovetsky Monastery were driven by the wind to their shore. The pilgrims saw the preparations for the construction work and began to help them zealously.

A wooden church was built on the place of the chapel and everything was prepared for it to be consecrated and to hold a service. Hieromonk Ephrem went to Vologda to visit the archbishop and ask him for an antimension and books for the new church. Having received everything required, he was coming back to the new cloister when Poles devastating the Russian land in that troubled time attacked and killed him. All church utensils were plundered. Cosmas and his son suffered the same fate: while collecting money for a church in the area of the Onezhskoe Lake, they were killed by Lithuanians in the Kargopolsky Uyezd. The other hermits left their cells; Sabbatios alone stayed at the hermitage.

The church remained unconsecrated for five years. Eventually the tombs of the venerated monks were visited by hieromonk Jacob. He consecrated the church in honour of the Transfiguration of the Lord and made a shrine on the place of the graves of the venerable Bassian and Jonah. Soon other hermits joined him. The new cloister was called the Pertominsky Monastery of the venerable Bassian and Jonah.

Peter I, caught by a storm on his way from the Solovetsky Monastery to Arkhangelsk, took refuge in the Pertominsky Monastery. He stayed there for three days and with his own hands made a huge wooden cross with the inscription in Russian and Dutch: "This cross was erected by the captain Peter in the summer of 1694". The cross was put on the shore and afterwards transferred to the cathedral of Arkhangelsk.

According to the "Solovetsky Patericon" (Moscow, 1906) the relics of the venerable Bassian and Jonah rest in the stone church of the Dormition of the Mother of God consecrated in 1691.

The finding of the relics of the venerable Bassian and Jonah is commemorated on June 5/18.

Their memory is celebrated on June 12/25.

Hermits of the XVIIth century

In the time of hegumen Anthony (1605-1612), Basil Kenozerts who liked living in seclusion in lonely parts of the island told his spiritual father Joseph about a meeting with the strange hermit Andrew: "Once I went far away from the monastery, I lost my way and was wandering about without food or water. Suddenly I saw something like the shadow of a man. I rushed towards it, but it disappeared in the forest; I kept running, saw a narrow path, followed it and it led me to the thickets where there was just a narrow passage for one person. I followed this passageway and came into the depth of the forest where I saw a mountain and the footprints of a barefooted man on it. I noticed a hole in the mountain. Having prayed I went into the cave. I crossed myself, stretched out my arms and touched a man, I became very frightened and said a prayer to which the inhabitant answered: "Amen". I fell at his feet. "Why have you come here? And what do you want?" asked the stranger. "Forgive me, holy father, I lost my way and came here; I beg you, take pity on me and tell me the way to the cloister". The hermit led me to another cave in which there was a window allowing light into the cave. Then I was able to see the stranger: he was naked, with a small beard, his body was black.

In the cave there were four logs with two boards put on them and two troughs; there was water in one trough and soaked grass in the other. The hermit gave me some grass and water. Having partaken of the offered food, I felt alive and strong. Then I asked the starets to tell me about his life. "I worked in the Solovetsky Monastery. My name is Andrew", he began, "Having come to the monastery, I worked in Sosnovaya and extracted salt. At that time the hegumen was Barlaam (1571-1581) who became metropolitan of Rostov afterwards.

The Hermit Andrew

"Soon sinful thoughts awoke in me and made me wish to leave everything and serve God. Without delay I left, found this place, dug out a cave and settled in it. I suffered from hunger and thirst; lived on berries and mushrooms, suffered demons' delusions, beating, abuse and illnesses. I struggled with my thoughts as with fierce animals. I regretted many times having left and considered my hermit's life futile. I even left the cave many times and wanted to go back to the world. But whenever I left the cave there would be a crash of thunder, a heavy shower would begin, and I had to come back in. Here, quiet coolness calmed me down. Several times I left the cave in winter, but an awful frost which made my bones crack did not let me take five steps. This hard struggle lasted for three years.

"After three years of temptations there came serenity and all hostile attacks ceased. Then somebody who looked like a saint appeared to me and said: "Lift up your spirits, do not abandon the path to God which has been shown to you." He gave me this grass saying: "Eat it and drink water from this lake". So I have been living on this grass for thirty eight years".

Having listened to this story I fell at the elder's feet asking for his prayers. Hermit Andrew led me out of the cave, showed me the way to the monastery, and blessed me saying: "Go in peace and do not tell anybody what you have heard from me until I am dead." I headed for the monastery and it seemed to me that it was just half a kilometre away from that place. After a while Basil and another disciple of Joseph's, Damian, set out in search of Andrew's cave; they walked for a week, but found neither the thickets nor the mountain with the cave.

Basil's narration impressed Damian very much. Wishing to lead an ascetic life, he was eager to speak to eremitic ascetics known only to God, therefore he spent forty days in the desert places of the island searching for the hermit. Eventually he became exhausted and hardly breathing lay under a tree. There the monks of the Monastery found him, put him on a stretcher, took him to the cloister and called his spiritual father. "What has happened to you, Damian?" asked his spiritual father. "Please forgive me, father, since I left the Monastery I have not seen any bread and ate only grass." Then Damian was given some bread and soon afterwards he recovered. But again the wish to find hermits awoke in him. After an assiduous prayer to God and the venerated Zosima and Sabbatios he left the monastery and this time found many hermits who were settled on the Solovetsky and Anzersky Islands. They were starets Ephrem the Black, layman Nicephore of Novgorod, Alexis of Kaluga, Joseph and Tikhon of Moscow, Theodoulos of Ryazan, Porphirios, Triphon, Joseph the Young, Sebastian and many others. Damian loved them with all his heart and began to visit them very often. When one of them died he buried him with his own hands.

Once during such work he was met by hermit Nicephore. "Visit, Damian, so that you could be visited by God", said the hermit and disappeared. In the desert Damian also found Timothy who during the Time of Troubles left his parents' house in Arkhangelsk, sailed to the island on a boat, built himself a hut and settled in it. Like Andrew he lived by eating grass.

Damian wished to follow the hermits' example, so he built himself a secluded cell and retired there to live in silence. But there he was overtaken by a great temptation. Once a monk who was serving Damian came to visit him, he said the prayer but did not receive a reply. The monk opened the door and found Damian hardly alive and all swollen. The hermit was taken to the Monastery hospital where he stayed for a while being looked after by experienced elders. But as soon as Damian recovered he decided to seek a new place of seclusion. He put out to sea on a small boat and settled near the Onega Lake. There he was beaten unmercifully by trappers; he recovered, left this location and went to Bodlo Lake where near the island, on Yuryev Mountain he erected a cross, built a cell and spent seven years there. Damian also began to build a church there dedicated to the Holy Trinity, but having made the foundations he died on November 27th 1633.

Except for these hermits of the wild forests on the Solovetsky Island, there were many other ascetics who sought salvation in the strictest silence. One of them was Adrian who lived near the lake in the middle of the island, two kilometres away from the cell built by hegumen Irenarch, and led a strict ascetic life; there he died and was buried in his hermitage.

The layman Sabbas, one of those who worked in the cloister, retired to the forest on the Solovetsky Island and lived there for eleven years being known only to God. Upon his death, in the days of hegumen Raphael, he was buried near Damian's cell (1633 - 1636). Near Sabbas' cell lived the hermit monk Nestor who spent day and night in prayer and fasting. When he died he was also buried near Damian's hermitage.

Nicephore, a son of the priest in Novgorod, came to the cloister when he was very young. He begged the superior to tonsure him, but his youth and beauty made the superior reject his request. The rejection only strengthened the young man's fervour to become a monk. Visitors from Novgorod passed him a letter from his parents in which they asked him to come back home as soon as possible. "Tell my parents", he answered the bearers of the letter, "that they will never see me again in this life, we will see each other only in the next world, after death".

Nicephore continued working for the monastery with others, keeping a strict fast; he would never lie down to sleep and would not rest long in a sitting position. In his spare time he liked reading the life of Mark of Thrace. The image of this hermit impressed him very much and attracted him to an eremitic life. Once, in the presence of all the workers, Nicephore jumped to his feet, crossed himself, took off his belt and sandals and, wearing just a long grey shirt, ran to the forest and stayed in seclusion on the Solovetsky Island for twelve years, fasting, praying and making prostrations. Then he was tonsured by a hermit. Having spent three years performing monastic feats he died as the flowers were beginning to blossom.

There were hermits whose names are known only to God. A monk of Solovki while travelling around the island attending to the needs of the cloister, became tired and wanted to have a rest near a steep mountain. Intending to lie on the ground he crossed himself and said the Jesus Prayer aloud. Suddenly he heard "Amen" from a cleft on the top of the mountain. He could not believe his ears and repeated the prayer several times and each time he heard the same "Amen".

"Who are you? A man or a spirit?" asked the monk with astonishment.

"I am a sinful man," answered the invisible voice, "and I mourn my sins."

"What is your name? And how did you come here?"

"Only God knows my name and how I came here."

"Are you here alone?"

"Two elders live near me; there was one more, but he passed away and we buried him."

"What do you eat?"

"Remember, brother, the Lord's words: man lives not only on bread but also on any word coming from God's mouth, it feeds and warms the inner man. Remember how in former times venerated men and women dwelled in mountains and in abysses. God the Creator fed them and is it not still the same God? If you want to know what the Lord feeds my transitory body with, try this."

With these words he threw a piece of something and the monk took it and ate. It was white moss ground with red whortleberries.

"This is what the Lord feeds me with", said the hermit. The monk began to implore him to say how many years he had lived there and how.

"I have lived here for ten or even more years", answered the hermit, "In the course of the first year I suffered much from demons' attacks. Demons would come in the form of robbers and threaten me: they would beat me unmercifully, drag me out of the cell and demand that I leave the island or go to the cloister. Having tortured me they would leave me barely alive. Then two holy men came to me with prosphora (the sacramental bread) in their hands. They said: "Stand up, brother, cross yourself and say the Jesus Prayer; do not be frightened of the crafty designs of the enemy, take courage, be strong, and God will help you: partake of this prosphora, we will be visiting you". Every time I ate the prosphora I would feel healthy and joyful.

In the course of the first year, when the demons' attacks were very bad, the elders visited me quite often; they would take me in the cave and heal me. The next year the demons' attacks became weaker, and now, with Christ's help, I am safe from all the enemy's attacks. But the elders sometimes visit me and bring me prosphora and bread".

When the monk was taking his leave, the hermit asked him to bring on a specified day some incense. The monk promised to do it, but he did not manage it on the specified day and later he could not find the hermit. The next year the monk went again to the place where he had talked to the hermit; being tired he lay down to have a rest. In his dream the hermit appeared and said: "Now you have come in vain", and gave him some prosphora.

The number of those who strived for an eremitic life was increasing, but living in seclusion without the guidance of spiritual fathers experienced in the inner struggle, they could yield to temptation. At that time Eleazar of Anzer started a skete (a community of hermits) intended for those who aspired to seclusion.

The venerable Irenarch, hegumen of the Solovetsky Monastery (+1628)

The venerated Irenarch made his monastic vows in the Solovetsky Monastery. In his life he tried to follow the example of the founders of the monastery, the venerated Zosima and Sabbatios. Upon the death of hegumen Anthony in 1614 he was appointed superior.

The humble and meek ascetic was constantly thinking of God. His monastic life was combined with service to his homeland. He put in a lot of effort to strengthen the defence of Byelomorye taking care of the protection of the monastery and the northern frontiers of Russia. According to the will of Tsar Michael Feodorovich the number of soldiers sustained by the monastery was increased to 1040. In Soumsky and Kemsky fortified towns, new defense installations were built. In 1621 under hegumen Irenarch a fortified building with two towers – Povarennaya and Kvasovarennaya – was constructed at the eastern wall of the Monastery.

The Tsar, knowing that the venerated hegumen was concerned about the brethren's spiritual life, by an official document ordered that the strict order of life in the monastery be maintained. The Tsar wrote: "... do not allow those who want to live in idleness, to take interest in worldly affairs and to have intoxicating drinks, to go out of the monastery and to talk too much, to do their will; see to it that the brethren live according to the holy fathers' rules and not by their own whims and that they go to church diligently. Let beginners be totally obedient to you, our faithful hegumen and to well-known elders..."

The venerable Irenarch, hegumen of the Solovetski Monastery

Under the spiritual guidance of the venerable Irenarch many ascetics grew spiritually in the cloister; among them was the venerable Eleazar, the founder of the Anzersky Skete. The place for the skete was determined by hegumen Irenarch himself who went with Eleazar to Anzer. Hegumen Irenarch not only gave his blessing to the monk Eleazar to build the skete on Anzer but also gave him the means to build and wrote about it to patriarch Philaret. The patriarch sent the official document approving the church construction and the Tsar's family donated church utensils.

Irenarch spent the last three years of his life in total silence having requested to be discharged from the office of superior. He passed away on July 17th 1628. His holy relics were buried by the brethren behind the altar of the Cathedral of the Transfiguration, on the northern side and a chapel was erected over them.

Being on Anzer, the venerable Eleazar foresaw the last hour of hegumen Irenarch's life and hurried to come to the main Solovetsky Island. At the same time Irenarch, seeing with inner sight his friend and associate, said that his spiritual brother Eleazar was coming by sea but that he would not arrive in time to pay his respects to him. Eleazar indeed arrived at the island when the hegumen Irenarch had already died.

The chapel in honour of the venerable Irenarch still exists. It is situated on the ground floor of the Holy Trinity cathedral.

The Solovetsky Patericon says also the following about Irenarch : In 1636 under hegumen Bartholomew, Marcel, the future hegumen of the Solovetsky Monastery and later archbishop of Vologodsk, was outside the monastery performing his obedience work and saw in his dream that he was standing in the Cathedral of the Transfiguration by the western wall and there were stairs to the big cupola. The venerated Irenarch came down these stairs, approached hegumen Bartholomew, took the staff from him and having said: "it is enough, brother, this is not your work " told Marcel to come up and take the staff.

Many inhabitants of the Dvinskaya land, Varzuga, of the fortified town of Soumsky, received help from hegumen Irenarch who saved them from perils at sea and bad weather in winter.

The memory of the venerable Irenarch is celebrated:

On July 17/30 – the day of commemoration of the venerable Irenarch, hegumen of the Solovetsky Monastery (1628)

On August 9/22 – the day of the celebration of the Synaxis of the Saints of Solovki

The venerable Eleazar, the founder of the Skete of the Holy Trinity on Anzer

Origin. Monasticism. The eremitic life on the Anzer island. Temptations. Schema. The foundation of the skete. Asceticism. Remarkable events. The construction of a wooden church. Eleazar's construction. Friendship with the venerable Irenarch. Becoming known to the Tsar. The Tsar's official document of 1633. Eleazar's disciples. Care for the construction of a stone church. Patriarch Nikon's care for the skete. Eleazar's experience of spiritual life. Death. Apparitions and miracles. Instructions to the monks about tonsure, the prayer rule, Holy Communion, burial. Teaching on Great Lent. The condition of the skete after Eleazar's death. The builders Nikodim and Roman. Joining the Solovetsky Monastery. The builder Spiridon. Finding of the venerable Eleazar's relics. Hegumen Melchisedech. The present condition of the skete

The venerable Eleazar is considered to be the organizer of an eremitic life on the Solovetsky Islands. Before him, hermits lived in seclusion in self-chosen places, but since he founded a skete they began to come to him, so the Anzer Skete of the Holy Trinity became a breeding-ground where lovers of an eremitic life were instructed.

Eleazar was born in the town of Kozelsk in the Kaluzhskaya Province at the end of XVIth century. His parents whose surname was Sevryukov belonged to the merchant class and were noted for their piety. Eleazar's inclination to a monk's life was discovered when he was very young. His pious parents did not want to prevent their son from fulfilling his good intention and gave him their blessing. Having come to the Solovetsky Monastery, Eleazar was accepted by hegumen Irenarch and began zealously and diligently to do the sculpturing in the Transfiguration Cathedral. By strict fasting, constant prayer and deep attention to his inner life the novice won the brethren's respect and the hegumen's love and was tonsured.

The venerable Eleazar of Anzer

Eleazar did not seek fame among people but strove for spiritual feats, so, having received hegumen Irenarch's blessing, he left the cloister and retired to the Anzersky Island, separated from the Solovetsky Island by a strait four km wide. At that time this island was uninhabited, only from time to time the White Sea ships and the monastery fishermen and trappers put in to its shore. In the middle of the island there was an extremely high mountain which is now called Golgotha. On a clear summer day from its top there is a majestic view of the vast waters, a big part of the Solovetsky and Muksalmsky Islands, the shore of the continent and the Zhizhguin Island. The whole Anzersky Island with its hills covered with thick pine and birch forests, with its lakes of different sizes, is situated below, as if at its feet.

Eleazar, charmed by the location, settled near the lake called the Round Lake. First of all he made and erected a wooden cross and built a hut near it. At first, life among wild animals and sea birds was hard for the hermit. He was attacked by demons many times. The demons would come to him in different aspects: either looking as acquaintances or warriors, unmounted or mounted, sometimes with weapons; they would violently attack Eleazar as if trying to kill him and would say: "Why have you come here? It is our place and nobody has ever come here before". "It is not yours," he would tell them, "but my Lord Christ's, and God wants me to live here". Then he would say the prayer: "Let God resurrect", and so would chase the uninvited visitors away. Sometimes they would come in various frightening forms with gnashing of teeth and howls; sometimes there would be sounds as thunderclaps or gunshots above his cell. But God consoled the ascetic by a joyous apparition: once when he was sitting in his cell the Most Holy Mother of God came to him and said:

"Take courage and be strong, the Lord is with you. Write on the cell walls: Christ, be with us". Then the Heavenly Queen gave him a staff and a rosary and became invisible. Another time he heard the singing: "I will glorify you, my Lord God, for you raised me and did not let my enemy torture me", and added: "Let the name of the Lord be blessed forever".

In order to earn his living the hermit made wooden cups and put them by the sea at the landing place: seafarers willingly took these cups and in exchange for them left bread and provisions. At some time in 1616, the monk Eleazar met the ascetic, the hieromonk Firs from the Solovetsky Monastery, and was tonsured a schema-monk by him. Having received the schema the hermit increased his feats, moved to another place of residence, to the bay, which is now called Trinity and which runs two km inland. There he found a dilapidated chapel and rebuilt it with his own hands. And as before he made wooden cups.

Soon the rumour about the hermit of Anzer spread over the White Sea shore and several others seeking silence and seclusion came to him. Eleazar decided not to withdraw from the people who like him were seeking to save their souls, but to organize a small community of hermits.

The venerable Eleazar established for his brethren an ancient type of eremitic life. All the hermits had a separate cell not far from each other, lived in it fasting and praying and making things to earn their living; they did not receive visitors and did not go anywhere and only came together for common prayer. This took place either in the chapel or in Eleazar's cell: in the evening they would celebrate Vespers, read the psalter, sing canons to the Lord Jesus and the Most Holy Mother of God, confess their thoughts and sins to their teacher; in the morning they would celebrate litya,

Matins, the Hours and then the ascetics would go to their cells to live in silence. Eleazar was a model of asceticism for all his disciples: he mortified his flesh by fasting, vigil and kneeling, wore iron chains, chopped firewood, and carried water. He devoted his spare time to copying useful books. The book of the skete says, "He collected many narratives from holy scripture; he wrote by hand three books of the Flower garden; he explained clearly the monastic prayer rule; he wrote for his brethren the rule of the skete as well as the lives of the elders and other books".

The following story demonstrates how Eleazar could overcome his desires: sometimes it happened that he felt he wanted to eat fish; then he would cook fish, put it in front of himself and, without touching it, reproach himself of intemperance. The untouched fish stayed in the cell and with time decomposed. Then the ascetic said to himself: "Now eat it if you want to".

The enemy could not stand such selflessness from the ascetic and became more and more angry with the venerated monk. Hegumen Irenarch of Solovetsky, having great respect for Eleazar, often visited him to have a spiritual conversation with him and invited him to the monastery, sending his invitation by a servant. Once his servant appeared with a horse and sleigh; having come to the window of the cell he gave the ascetic the regards from the hegumen and passed the invitation on to visit the monastery. Eleazar began to prepare for the journey and performed the morning prayer earlier than usual. Having noticed that the servant would often leave the cell during the service he asked him: "Why do you often go out of the cell?" "I go out to have a look at the house to check whether it is quiet", was the answer. After prayers Eleazar wanted to have a meal and suggested that the visitor join him;

before eating he as usual began to say the Lord's Prayer, but as soon as he pronounced: "And lead us not into temptation, but deliver us from evil", the pretended servant immediately disappeared. The ascetic looked with terror through the window but did not see any traces of his visitor. Then he realized that it was the devil's temptation and thanked the Lord God who had not let the enemy mock him. Sometimes the enemy of humanity set evil people against Eleazar. Once he got some inhabitants of the seashore to rob the ascetic, having suggested to them that he was very rich. These people arrived at the island and came to the poor cell of the elder who, foreseeing their intention, began to pray to God to protect him. The villains did not manage to do anything and as if having become mad began to run wildly around the cell. Taking pity upon them Eleazar went out of his cell and asked them: "Why have you come? And what do you want?" But the miserable people could not answer and kept going round. Then the ascetic prayed God to deliver them from the invisible bonds and his prayer was heard; the villains came to their senses, repented and asked the elder forgiveness. He forgave them and, having told them not to want other people's property, let them go home.

Though the ascetic tried hard to avoid fame, he became known even to the Tsar's family. When during the reign of Michael Feodorovich hegumen Irenarch was in Moscow on monastery business, the mother of the Tsar, the great staritsa (female of starets) Martha Ivanovna received him. During the conversation the aged nun asked him: "Is it true that hermits live on the Anzersky Island?" When the hegumen answered in the affirmative, the staritsa suggested constructing a church for them and donated 100 rubles for this purpose. The hermits of the Anzersky Island themselves had wanted to build a church, but had not had enough money and had not known how to begin the construction. Now they saw that God was taking care of them and had suggested this idea to the Tsar's mother. Another event helped the hermits of the Anzersky Island to fulfill their wish even more. The elder Alexander Bulatnikov, the successor of the famous cellarer of the Troitsko-Serguieva Lavra, Abraham Palitsyn, respected by the Tsar and all his family, knew Eleazar. Together with hegumen Irenarch he informed patriarch Philaret about the construction of the Anzer Skete and the absence of a church there. On March 18th 1620, by an official document, the patriarch ordered the hegumen of the Solovetsky Monastery, Irenarch, to send some carpenters to the skete to build a church dedicated to the Holy Trinity with a side-chapel to the venerated Michael the Small and promised to present icons, utensils, books and everything else necessary for the divine service. As far as the Tsar is concerned, by an official document of January 20th 1621, he ordered that the hermits of the Anzersky Island be sustained by the Solovetsky Monastery without interfering in the management of the monastery grounds, be in obedience to the superior of the Solovetsky Monastery and that the elders not do anything unauthorized, not receive lay people and avoid talk and disturbance.

After the church had been built the hermits of the Anzersky Island did not leave their cells but began to gather more often for common worship. Hieromonk Barlaam would celebrate the divine service for them and as head of the skete exercised some power over the hermits. Eleazar himself avoided being in charge of the skete and remained a spiritual father and an advisor of the brethren. Soon afterwards however, in 1624, probably according to the Tsar's or the patriarch's will he had to take on this burden and become the head; the new position became even harder for him when his patron and friend, hegumen Irenarch of Solovetsky, reposed. The following incident shows what spiritual capacities both ascetics gained: when Irenarch was dying, Eleazar, being in his skete, told the brethren: "My friend and brother, hegumen Irenarch, is dying today and I shall hurry to the cloister but I will not find him alive". Irenarch, being on his deathbed, told the brethren of the Solovetsky Monastery: "Today my spiritual brother Eleazar is leaving his skete for our cloister and wishes to arrive before my death, but according to God's will he will not see me alive".

Under Macarios, the new hegumen of the Solovetsky Monastery, by the official document of February 7th 1628, it was determined that the number of brethren in the Anzersky Skete should be twelve and it was ordered that for this number of monks the following would be allocated from the finances of the Dvinskaya province, via the Solovetsky Monastery: 2 rubles per person for clothing, 600 litres of rye flour, 100 litres of oats and malt, 50 litres of cereals and oat flour for food, 16 kg, three buckets of red wine, ten pounds of incense on church expenses, 200 litres of wheat flour for prosphoras and 5 rubles for firewood . Thanks to this care of Tsar Michael Feodorovitch the hermits of Anzer were well provided for. The Tsar's favour towards the Anzer Skete became even greater after a certain happy event in the Tsar's family. During a conversation with Alexander Bulatnikov the Tsar expressed his sorrow that he did not have an heir and asked: "Who could pray to God to cure us of our sterility?" "There is an ascetic in your country", answered the elder, "whose prayer can be heard by God", and he told the Tsar about the life and feats of the venerable Eleazar. The pious Tsar was happy to hear this piece of news and sent a messenger to invite the hermit to Moscow. Eleazar arrived in Moscow and during the first conversation with him the Tsar revealed the aim of his invitation. Consoling the tsar the ascetic said: "Due to your faith God will not leave you without an heir to the throne". The sovereign took these words as a prophecy and asked the elder to stay in the Chudov Monastery and wait. Soon the Lord consoled the Tsar by giving him a son, Alexis (1629). The birth of the Tsarevitch (the Tsar's son) brought joy and celebration to the Tsar's house. The Tsar did not forget the hermit of Anzer who was staying in the Chudov Monastery. He called Eleazar and offered him honours and holy orders, but the humble ascetic refused this flattering offer intending to end his life in solitude.

Out of respect for the founder of the Anzer Skete the Tsar wanted to improve the position of the skete and by the official document of July 31st 1633, declared the Anzersky Skete independent of the monastery and allowed the hermits to elect administrators from their own community, to have twelve brethren and two laymen to chop firewood, not to send defaulters to the Solovetsky Monastery to be corrected but to reclaim them at their own discretion. The hegumen of the Solovetsky Monastery was ordered not to assume administration of the skete, not to send any administrators there, not to oppress the hermits in any way and not to prevent the monastery brethren from going to the skete and stay there if this was their wish. The governor of Dvinskaya province was ordered by the Tsar's special document of July 31st 1633, under threat of disfavour, to send the allotted maintenance to the Anzer Hermitage directly, not through the Solovetsky Monastery, on state carts and ships in proper time and in its entirety. Nevertheless the envy and malevolence of evil people gave the hermits much trouble and sorrow. On July 13th 1634, some malefactors came to the island with the obvious purpose of robbery, but at that time coast-dwellers' boats put in to the mouth of the bay and the robbers having become frightened fled. After the complaint of Eleazar, the Tsar by the official document of January 31st 1638, ordered the governor of Soumy to guard the skete against robbers and evil-doers.

At that time some remarkable people joined the skete. In 1634 came Nicodemos; soon afterwards he became Eleazar's favourite disciple and after his death he became his successor. Nicetas, a priest from Moscow arrived, in search of a strict ascetic life. After a short time he made his monastic vows and received the name of Nikon. In feats of fasting and praying Nikon's ardent soul matured in the Anzer Skete for his future work as metropolitan of Novgorod and then as patriarch of all Russia. Every day Nikon would read the Psalter, the canons to the Lord Jesus Christ and the Mother of God and would make thousand prostrations. This new ascetic however, was not long an inspiring example for the skete brethren as God's Providence was leading him to a higher service and Nikon moved to Kozheezerskaya hermitage.

The old church became too small for the increasing number of brethren and the venerated Eleazar decided to build a stone church in honour of the Annunciation of the Most Holy Mother of God, 11 m in size. There were almost enough means saved in the course of time; as a last resort they could rely on the charity of some coast-dwellers. The hermits appealed to the Tsar with a petition to build a stone church and soon after received his permission. The pious Tsar showed the greatest concern for this undertaking to the glory of God, and ordered the governor of the Dvinskaya province, Prince Lvov, to allocate 200 rubles for this construction from the customs fees, so that the hermits of Anzer would pray to God for the peace of the soul of his father, Patriarch Philaret. Besides, the Tsar ordered Lvov to send builders and bricklayers to the skete. Hegumen Bartholomew of the Solovetsky Monastery was ordered by the official document of January 12th 1638, to give the hermits bricks and lime from the monastery brickyard for the construction of the church as well as the money belonging to the Anzer Skete which had been granted by the Tsar.

But this good intention would not be realized soon. Hegumen Bartholomew of Solovetsky did not like Eleazar's undertaking and reported to Moscow that the construction of the church conceived by the head of the Anzer Skete was beyond their means, and that there were no materials available in the monastery. Although the next year Bartholomew deserted the position of superior, the construction of the stone church was delayed for an uncertain time. The venerable Eleazar had to endure much trouble and distress. In spite of this he did not despond and did not give up his intention. Eight years later the following event helped him to begin the construction. Alexis Mikhailovich, having assumed the throne at his father's death, remembered the hermit of Anzer who had predicted his birth and wished to see him. In spite of his age Eleazar went to the capital and was graciously received by the sovereign. The Tsar presented him the official document of February 11th 1646, that confirmed his approval of the construction, and ordered Elias, hegumen of the Solovetsky Monastery to build the stone church of a determined size in the skete and to officially inform prince Lvov about the estimated cost of the construction. Now all the obstacles seemed to have been removed; hegumen Elias, however, did not proceed with the construction until he received the confirmation of the Tsar's will from the governor of Dvinskaya Province, prince Romodanovsky. Meanwhile, being angry with Eleazar, he kept him for some time imprisoned in the Solovetsky Monastery.

Finally the ascetic was able not only to see the successful construction of the church but also to direct it and take part in it. So when in the early spring, bricks were not delivered from the monastery and the workers could not work, in spite of the fact that ice blocks were drifting in the sea Eleazar himself and several people sailed on a boat to the monastery. They loaded the boat with bricks and lime but on their way back they were trapped by the ice. The danger was great but Eleazar did not lose heart and trusted in God, he took the helm and saved everybody from death. Due to the zealous labour of Eleazar and his brethren the stone church of the skete with a refectory and cells for the hermits was built, but it was consecrated only after the death of the venerable Eleazar.

At the time that the hermit of Anzer was enduring all these hardships his former brother, Nikon, metropolitan of Novgorod, and later patriarch of all Russia, was his help and support. Nikon remembered the Anzersky Skete where he had made his monastic vows and concluded almost each letter to the authorities of Solovki with the words: "and for the sake of God we ask you to regard with favour the elders of Anzer and to take care of them"; or: "Take care of the elders of Anzer, the founder and the brethren, and we will be happy to help you if we can". Nikon tried to fulfil any request of his former teacher. So, in 1651, in a letter to archimandrite Elias of the Solovetsky Monastery, the metropolitan wrote the following: "Starets Eleazar and the brethren of the Anzersky Skete humbly ask permission for the elder Cyricos from the hospital to leave the Solovetsky Monastery and go to the Anzer

Skete. So as soon as you receive this letter let Starets Cyricos go to the Anzer Skete". Having become patriarch, Nikon helped the Anzer Skete with even more eagerness. By the official document of April 29th 1655 he informed them that according to his petition the Tsar ordered to increase the donation for the Anzer Skete and to give it 16 kg of incense, 48 kg of beeswax, 5 buckets of church wine, 800 litres of wheat flour for prosphoras; to add 1 ruble for the head and the brethren and to give money to the newly arrived monks. In addition the patriarch personally donated 2 rubles to Eleazar and 11 rubles to the brethren, 1 ruble per person. Some time later the patriarch sent silver covering frames for icons, 250 rubles in cash, 11 sturgeons for the brethren and a beluga sturgeon for Eleazar asking for prayers both communal and private.

Taking care of his skete and doing his best to improve it, Eleazar was approaching his death. He committed to paper the experience of his spiritual life and thus preserved it for all those seeking salvation.

"Once I was standing in front of the icon of Christ the Saviour and praying with tears: O Lord Christ, King and Creator! What will I render to You for Your mercy on me? I have done nothing good for You", and I saw a dove touching my face and say: "I will bring your tears to God", then it disappeared. After that my soul rejoiced'.

"When our brother Tikhon reposed, another brother, also Tikhon by name, took stealthily two books that had belonged to the deceased. The time for the evening prayer came. Four brethren came to the church. Suddenly I saw some divine force in the form of a dove above each monk's head, only Tikhon did not have it. I was greatly surprised but could not understand the meaning of it. Soon, however, the defaulter came up to me and repenting with tears of his misdeed asked forgiveness."

"When I was deeply depressed because of many hardships and even wanted to leave the Anzer Skete, I would hear a mysterious voice: "Do not be frightened, the Lord is with you ", or "In your patience possess ye your souls" (Luke 21:19), or: "We then that are strong ought to bear the infirmities of the weak" (Romans 15:1). I did not trust such apparitions in order not to fall in the devil's delusion. But my disbelief disappeared when I had the following vision: I was standing in my cell and looking through the window, when I heard an awful thunderclap, though the sky was blue, and the reproaching words from the Gospel: "O faithless and perverse generation, how long shall I be with you? How long shall I suffer you?" (Mathew 17:17).

At the same hard time for me, I also had the following vision: I was standing in a beautiful valley. Somebody came up to me and pointing to the sky said: "Look!" Having looked I saw an unusually light ray resembling a rainbow and spreading over the whole sky. After a while the stranger said again: "Look at the sky!" I obeyed and saw in the ineffable light the images of the Lord Jesus Christ, the Most Holy Mother of God, John the Baptist and two Apostles. Finally the luminous young man said for the third time: "Look at the sky!" I looked up again and saw a wonderful image of Christ the Saviour of an unusual size. Then the stranger reproached me my faintheartedness and lack of patience for the sake of Him who endured everything for us, and disappeared".

"Once when as usual I was saying the Jesus Prayer and making prostrations in my cell, I also began to pray to the Most Holy Mother of God: "O Most Holy Lady Mother of God, save me, a sinner!" Suddenly the Most Holy Mother of God appeared in front of me, in the radiance of heavenly glory with three stars – one on the head and two on the shoulders. The Heavenly Queen said: "Eleazar, keep calling upon Me in your prayers and I will help you until your soul leaves the earth".

"During Lent on a weekday I was honoured to see the Heavenly Queen standing opposite Her icon, near the left choir, facing the church. When, having left both choirs, we came to the middle of the church and began to sing: "All creation rejoices in You, O Blessed one", the Most Holy Lady left Her place, stood in front of us and stayed there until we finished singing.

Another time in the Church of the Holy Trinity the Heavenly Queen came to me as She is depicted on the Smolenskaya Icon, having the Child Jesus on Her left arm, and said: "Eleazar, keep Christ's commandments and build a church dedicated to Me". With these words the vision disappeared".

Once in the same church the Apostle Paul with the Icon of Our Lady of the Sign in his right hand appeared to me and said: "Eleazar, when you come to the church, bow to the icon of Christ the Saviour with fear and trembling; tell the brethren this".

"Once I asked myself a question: what God-pleasing deeds do I do? And what is the meaning of my work and prayer? Then I prayed zealously: "O Lord God, Father Almighty, instruct me how to glorify Your all-holy name!" After this prayer I heard the heavenly voice: "Pray every day, saying: Glory be to God on high, and on earth peace and good will towards men... O Lord, You have been our refuge... Vouchsafe O Lord, to keep us this day without sin".

The Venerable Eleazar signed his narrative about these wonderful appearances with the words: "by the sinful elder Eleazar".

On January 13th 1656, the Anzer Hermitage lost its founder and organizer Eleazar. His death was preceded by a brief and slight illness caused by old age and exhaustion. On his deathbed the elder talked to his disciples advising them to live virtuously, not to break the rules and pious customs of the hermitage, and promising them God's blessed help. Finally the ascetic appointed his successor in charge of the brethren – his disciple and associate Nikodemos, and having received communion, peacefully passed away.

The visions and wonderful help received by people proved that Eleazar had obtained God's grace. One monk, Onuphry was once so cast down that he became ill and lost his reason. At the moment of his most excruciating sufferings Eleazar appeared to him, prayed for him and immediately healed him.

Once hieromonk Ismael of Anzer fell so badly ill that he could not leave his cell and he took to his bed. Being completely exhausted he fell asleep and had a vision in which the venerable Eleazar went out of his chapel and approached his cell. The monk awoke and having forgotten about his illness got up from his bed and hurried to the window to see if what he had seen was true. After that he recovered.

The monk Macarios from the same hermitage, a skillful painter, decided to paint the venerable Eleazar but he did not know what he looked like. Being upset about this the monk did his evening prayer and went to bed. Suddenly he saw Eleazar who said: "Brother, you wanted to see me, so now I am standing before you". The monk awoke in fear and saw Eleazar in reality. Then Macarius fell on his knees and bowed before Eleazar; who after that disappeared. The monk kept his appearance in mind and painted him.

Once Isaiah, a virtuous man and the head of the Anzer Hermitage at that time, had to go to the Solovetsky Monastery. Though it was winter, the strait separating the Solovetsky from from the Anzersky island was free from ice: Isaiah and another monk sailed in a small boat. On their way back they were caught by blocks of ice drifting from the sea. The huge blocks of ice surrounded the boat and carried it to the open sea. Terrified the travellers got out of the boat on the ice and rushed to the coast. Isaiah stumbled and nearly died. At that moment Eleazar appeared to him and saved him from death. The coast of Anzer, the travellers' destination, was still far away and the drifting blocks of ice were carrying them in the opposite direction; to make matters worse night fell. Being exhausted they appealed to God with a zealous prayer to deliver them from danger and began to call upon Eleazar beseeching him to help them. Soon in the dim light of the moon they saw the venerable Eleazar standing at the opposite side of the ice-floe and navigating it to the Anzersky Island. Happy to see him the monks wanted to approach him and bow before him but he disappeared. Meanwhile the ice-floe reached the coast of the Anzersky Island and the travellers went ashore safely.

In order to understand Eleazar's idea of monasticism better and the way he guided others in monastic feats, we think it useful to give a brief account of his precepts to newly-tonsured monks. In these precepts he first teaches generally about faith, morality and repentance. Then he draws the monk's attention to the vows he has made and describes the first degree of monasticism, how the monk is entrusted to the elder and performs works of obedience. Then he expounds on nightly temptations and adds various views on keeping the body pure. After that he gives instructions about demons' nightly attacks. There is also a special precept about sharing a cell with a brother. The rest of the rules consist of extracts from the precepts to monks of St. Ephrem and Isaac the Syrian and some others.

The precepts of the venerable Eleazar introduce us to the rules and customs of the monastic life of that time. So according to the precepts the aspirant monk comes to the hermitage, falls at the feet of the superior and pleads with him and the brethren to accept him in the community. The superior orders him to stay in the monastery and work for the sake of God with other workers and watches his diligence and faith. Having made certain of his zeal and good intentions the superior consults the brethren and appoints the day of the Tonsure. The novice hears this with joy. He is taken to a special cell and told to spend the night in vigil. The superior chooses from among the brethren an elder who will guide the newly-tonsured monk. The chosen elder beseeches the superior not to entrust him with such responsibility as he thinks that he himself needs guidance. The superior reproves him for disobedience and the elder obeys. He asks the Superior's blessing saying: "Through your holy prayers may the Lord preserve and deliver us from the devil's crafty designs and put us on the right path". Then they bring the novice to the church, take his secular clothes off and the superior puts a loose-fitting long robe on him. They put the lectern in front of the holy gates and put the Gospel and scissors on it, then they lead the novice to the left side of the lectern. After that the superior or the priest administers the Tonsure as prescribed. As soon as the rite is finished the monk is placed to the left of the holy gate with the Gospel in his hands, and the brethren, kissing the Gospel, ask the new monk what is his monastic name; he says his name. The brethren say: "Save your soul and pray God for the tsar". The monk replies: "God saves and has mercy". Then they take the Gospel from him. The superior calls the elder and having taken the newly-tonsured monk by his right hand, entrusts him to the elder with the following words: "Brother, you receive a brother to be obedient to you, he is pure due to the holy Gospel; not only his sins are wiped out, but also his secular name is wiped out and a new name is written in heaven. You receive him pure so place him pure before God and humbly teach him the Jesus Prayer, obedience and all the monastic rules; and you, brother, accept this elder, be obedient to him until death, do not contradict him in anything, always remember the vows you have made for God. If you are good, you will obtain grace from God, blessing from us, and prayers from your elder. If you break the monastery rule, you will be punished". After this admonition the elder and the monk receive a blessing from the superior and go to the church of the Wonder-workers; having performed the usual prayer rule there, the elder leads the monk to his cell, where he says: "Truly it is meet to bless you...". Then according to the prayer rule they do the Hours and burn incense in front of the icons. After that he teaches him the Jesus Prayer and instructs him to lead a monastic life according to Holy Scripture, to keep his soul pure before God, to obey the superior, to have spiritual love for everyone; he shows him the place in the cell where he should do the prayer rule, where he should stand and so on. When the church bell rings the elder takes the monk to the cathedral to the place for newly-tonsured monks and, receiving a blessing from the superior asks him where the new monk should stand. He begins to pray with him, watches him or stands next to him giving detailed instructions about the common prayer rule. After the liturgy the elder goes with the monk to the refectory, puts him among the newly-tonsured monks and according to the cellarer's instruction places him at the table and gives him a piece of prosphora; the elder teaches the monk to keep silence and to pray silently, to drink and eat moderately what is given and only after receiving the elder's blessing. He instructs him that when he goes to or comes back from the cathedral he should not stand on the territory of the monastery, he should not hang about, he should not talk to anybody or look at anything, but he should go his way and keep his veil lowered. When they come back to the cell the elder teaches the monk the prayer rule and allows him to have a rest. The elder receives the necessary vestments from the treasurer and does his prayers, prostrations and the entire prayer rule together with the monk until he learns how to do it. For those who can read, the prayer rule contains the following: the Canon to Jesus, the Canon to the Mother of God, to the Guardian Angel, to the Wonder-workers, the evening prayers, the night prayers, four kathismas from the Book of Psalms, the Hours, 300 prostrations, 600 Jesus Prayers: "Lord Jesus Christ, Son of God, have mercy on me, a sinner", and 100 prayers to the Mother of God: "Lady Mother of God, have mercy on me, a sinner", as well as prayers for the Tsar and his House, for the army, for the metropolitan, for the Father Superior, for the spiritual father, for the praying mentor, for the brethren in the same cell and the other brethren, for those in service and work, for the sick and for those who care for them, for those who do wrong and those who forgive them, for relatives and all Orthodox believers.

This praying rule begins with the following: "God, cleanse me from my sins and have mercy on me" (prostration). "You who created me, a sinner, have mercy on me" (prostration). "I have sinned much, O Lord, forgive me" (prostration). "It is truly meet to bless you, Mother of God, ever blessed and most pure and mother of our God. More honorable than the Cherubim, and beyond compare more glorious than the Seraphim, incorruptibly you gave birth to God the Word. We magnify you, truly Theotokos", "Unto You we ascribe glory, to the Father and to the Son and to the Holy Spirit, now and ever, and unto the ages of ages. Lord, have mercy upon us". (three times). "Lord, bless me. Lord Jesus Christ, Son of God, through the prayers of Your most pure Mother and of the Holy Guardian Angel and of our venerated and God-bearing fathers Zosima and Sabbatios and of all the saints, have mercy on us, amen". "Glory to You, our God, glory to You!" (three times). "God, cleanse me, sinner, and have mercy on me, for I have sinned against you, deliver me from evil, Your will be done and open my lips to praise Your Holy name the Father, the Son and the Holy Spirit, now and ever, and unto the ages of ages, amen". Then: "Heavenly King, Comforter, Spirit of truth, who are present everywhere fills all things, Treasury of good things and Giver of life, come and dwell in us. Cleanse us of every stain, and save our souls, gracious Lord", "Holy God, Holy and Mighty, Holy Immortal, have mercy on us", the Lord's prayer, "Lord, have mercy," 12 times, "Come and let us worship", Psalm 50, The Symbol Of Faith".

Those who cannot read, must do the following rule every day: 3000 Jesus Prayers, 300 prayers to the Mother of God, 300 prostrations and prayers for the Tsar and others. The elder, first of all, should teach the illiterate monk the Jesus Prayer, the Prayer of Forgiveness, and "Truly it is meet to bless you...". In general he should take care of the monk entrusted to him as of his own soul, he should watch his life, instruct him and not allow any transgressions for what the monk learns at this stage he will abide by later. Without the elder's permission the monk should neither take nor give anything, neither learn from anyone nor talk to anyone. When the Lord honours him to receive Communion, the brethren bid farewell to each other in the cell, then come to the church of the Wonder-workers, say the prayers, bid farewell to the Wonder-workers and kiss their relics. During the liturgy the sacristan installs the lectern with the icon of the Theotokos on it; the brethren bid farewell to the superior one by one, then kiss the icon of the Saviour and the icon of the Theotokos, making two prostrations before kissing and one after, then they approach the Holy Mysteries two by two. When the superior comes through the holy gates with the Holy Communion, they make three prostrations and receive the Holy Communion bare-headed. After receiving the Communion, they put their klobuk back on and receive a prosphora, wash their mouth and hands above a bowl and wipe themselves with a towel.

As far as the burial of a monk is concerned it is said in the rule that all the brethren should be present if no emergency prevents them. First they kiss the deceased on the lips, then they kiss the icon which is placed on him. After the burial they make fifteen prostrations saying: "Give rest, Lord, to the soul of Your servant, our monk (name) who has fallen asleep, in Your Kingdom, where there is no pain, sorrow or suffering. In Your goodness and love for all men, forgive all the sins he has committed in thought, word or deed, for there is no man who lives and sins not, You only are without sin.

For You are the Resurrection, the Life, and Repose of Your servant (name), departed from this life, O Christ our God; and to You we ascribe glory with Your Eternal Father and Your All-holy, Good and Life-giving Spirit; both now and forever and to the ages of ages. Amen.

The monk's life is a life of constant fasting and praying; but the forty days of Great Lent have always been notable for the intensification of the feats. During the cheese-fare week after the Matins the superior gives the brethren the following instructions: "God's servants, elders and all the brethren, the time of the holy Great Lent approaches and we must prepare ourselves for the spiritual feats of lent, having ceased all dark, evil, sinful deeds and dressed ourselves in light and thus being prepared, we must do pious feats of fasting and abstinence. Our Lord and God himself kept a forty days fast, though he had committed no sin, thereby giving us an example; we, sinful, and guilty of so many sins before God, must refrain from all that is evil and beseech God to forgive us and take care of our souls. And you, virtuous elders and brethren, for the love of God, spend Great Lent in purity, abstinence and feats; sincerely confess your sins to your spiritual fathers and pray the all-bountiful God, in private and in public, for health and salvation of the soul of our Sovereign, faithful and pious Tsar and Great Prince (name) of all Russia and His faithful Tsarina and Great Princess (name), their faithful children (name), their princes and boyars, and all Orthodox Christians, so that the Lord will grant welfare to our Tsar and all his country. And pray God to forgive your sins, so that the all-gracious God will deliver us from eternal sufferings. And if you feel animosity or anger towards someone, for the love of God, forgive him, for we are granted forgiveness of our sins by forgiving our brothers. If we do not forgive them, we will not be forgiven: "For with the same measure that ye mete withal it shall be measured to you again" (Luke 6:38). You should come at the very beginning of the Service and listen to it attentively. And make mention of us, sinners, in your holy prayers, and we bless you". The brethren would usually reply: "We will do our best, virtuous father, to act in this manner following your order", and bow before the Superior.

Upon Eleazar's death his disciple Nicodemos was in charge of the Anzer Hermitage for 21 years, managing the hermitage in the spirit of his teacher. The payment which patriarch Nikon informed the monks of the hermitage about in 1655, was confirmed by the Tsar's edict of 1662. We do not have any information about the influence which the disturbances in the Solovetsky Monastery, caused by the correction of the divine service books, had on the life of the Anzer Hermitage, except for a brief note made in the book of the Anzer Hermitage in 1710: "When disturbances started on the Solovetsky Island and the enemies of the monastery laid siege to it, the Anzer Hermitage suffered from the devastation and desolation. The hermits who lived there were all banished, they fled, and all the churches were robbed, only walls remained, all the church utensils and books were carried away and some of them were lost; only after a long time did the Solovetsky Monastery manage to return some of the church items and books".

This appropriation of the church property of the Anzer Hermitage, however, took place after the suppression of the revolt on the Solovetsky Island. The reason for that might have been the repentance of the monk Metrophan who had fled from the Solovetsky Monastery during its siege. He said that it was the Anzer Hermitage that supplied wine and fish to the Solovetsky Monastery during its siege. In 1667 when Nicodemos died, following the decree of patriarch Joseph, the Anzer Hermitage was deprived of its icons, church vessels, books, chasubles, official documents and 494 rubles of money. But at the instance of the head of the hermitage Roman, Tsar Theodore Alekseyevich ordered to return all that had been appropriated and resume the payment to the hermitages. In 1685 when Roman was in

Moscow the Tsar granted him many endowments for the Anzer skete.

Before that the hermitage had been independent of the Solovetsky Monastery and this independence had been confirmed by the Tsar's edict many times. In 1682 by the decree of archbishop Athanasios of Cholmogory, the hermitage was placed under the jurisdiction of the archimandrite of the Solovetsky Monastery who was ordered to supervise and command the hermits at his own discretion. In 1698 archbishop Athanasios established the post of treasurer because of the dilapidation of the bell tower and cells of the hermitage, and in 1700 Tsar Peter ordered instead of paying for the board for 17 monks and for church expenses to give 145 rubles at the end of each year. So it is evident that the hermitage did not prosper at that time. In about 1705 the writer narrating the life of the venerable Eleazar complained that the memory of the founder of the hermitage had been almost wiped out and his tomb was rarely visited. It is unknown what this condition of the hermitage could have led to, but there came a man who restored the eremitic life in the Anzer Hermitage, revived the memory of its founder and started a new refuge for hermits on the mountain Golgotha. That was Job, Jesus by his monastic name, in the world a priest in Moscow, John Ioannov, the Tsar's confessor; we will tell about him below.

Under the founder Spiridon a new wooden church was built and the stone church dedicated to the Holy Trinity was repaired. The spiritual achievements of that time, however, are unknown. In 1757 when the foundations for a chapel dedicated to the venerable Eleazar were being dug, four coffins were found, one of them with the cover intact; the body in it was incorrupt, only the clothes had decayed; the coffin was emitting fragrance.

The monks of the Anzer Hermitage concluded that it was the coffin of the venerable Eleazar, the founder of the hermitage, and reported about it to the archbishop of Arkhangelsk, Barsanuphy. By the decree of August 16th 1758, the archbishop ordered the head of the Anzer Hermitage, Melchisedech and the brethren to put the coffin into a new grave inside the chapel; the grave was to be covered by beams or a stone vault and the shrine sent by the archbishop was to be put over it, surrounded by an iron railing and covered by a special cloth; during the transfer of the relics the thanksgiving service to the venerable Eleazar was to be celebrated. Later, the wooden chapel built over the grave in 1757 was replaced by a stone chapel, and this century, the former ramshackle shrine was replaced by a new one made of brass and silver.

In 1762 bishop Joseph of Arkhangelsk, was visiting his flock and came to the Anzer Hermitage. He installed Melchisedech, the head of the hermitage as Superior and wished this title always to be attributed to the heads of the Anzer Hermitage. Joseph decreed to read daily the Akathist to the Mother of God before the wonder-working icon of the Sign and to hold a thanksgiving service before the wonder-working icon of the Holy Trinity on feast days. In 1764 the Anzer Hermitage was attached to the Solovetsky Monastery; it was to have its own head and twelve monks. Now those monks of the Solovetsky Monastery who seek silence may go to the hermitage if they receive the Superior's blessing.

They celebrate the daily services according to church rules and they also follow the special monastic rule: three canons after the Vespers – to the Sweetest Jesus, the Mother of God, the Guardian Angel, and the Akathist as well as prayers before sleeping and prayers with prostrations for all who help the monastery by their charity.

Besides this, each monk has his cell rule with prostrations and the Jesus Prayer.

Hieroschemamonk Job, founder of the Golgotha-Crucifixion Hermitage

Origin. Priesthood. Visitors. Love for beggars. Court life. Visiting prisons. Seclusion at home. Illness. Slander. Retiring to the Solovetsky Monastery. Obedience. Temptation. Moving to the Anzer Hermitage. Appointment as head of the hermitage. Teaching the brethren. The order in the hermitage. Serving the sick. Schema. The appearance of the Most Holy Mother of God. Moving to Golgotha. The foundation of the hermitage. The construction of the church. Donations of royalty. The letters of Tsaritsa Maria. The attack of the robbers. The increase of the number of hermits. Job's feats. Rule of the hermitage. The appearance of the Most Holy Mother of God. Miracles. Illness. Forgiveness. Death. Burial. The condition of the hermitage upon Job's death. Joining to the Anzer Hermitage. Joining the Solovetsky Monastery. The construction of the stone church. The present condition of the hermitage.

Job was born in Moscow during the reign of Tsar Michael Fyodorovich in 1635 and called John. There is no information about his parents and his early upbringing, except for the fact that his father's name was also John. He is said to have come from the clergy and to have been brought up according to the rules of morals and piety, so as soon as he came of age he was ordained to the priesthood. When he became priest his inborn aspiration to a virtuous life was realized to the fullest. He would hold divine services every day and would often stand in the choir and sing. His singing was naturally sweet and touching. Father Job's touching and devout way of celebrating attracted many people to his church;

people also were eager to come to his house after the service to receive his blessing and to get to know him. He was not vain, however, and did not accept such visitors willingly and often did not satisfy their curiosity to see him at home.

Hieroschemamonk Job (schema monk Jesus)

Father John, becoming more and more virtuous, would not only fulfill the priestly prayer rule but also the monastic one, thus staying in the world he led a monastic life. He would often oblige himself to fast and live in seclusion and shut himself in his bedroom where he would spend nights on his knees praying to God. During these nightly prayers John would call on God with tears: "O Lord, have mercy on me, O Lord spare me, etc". In the morning he would reluctantly interrupt his seclusion and go to church. Sometimes John's servants, at the demand of some visitors would inform him that guests had come to receive his blessing and advice before the service. Forced by those insistent requests he would receive the visitors but with a sad face, while on other occasions he would receive visitors with sincere love and would talk to them open-heartedly. Educating everyone in Christian virtues he could adjust his speech to the status, title and condition of every person. With older people he talked about praying, with young people about the danger of passions and whims, with fathers about the upbringing of children in fear of God and so on. He based all his sermons on the Holy Scriptures and added to them examples from church history and the lives of the saints. He liked to visit his friends and acquaintances; sometimes he would come to someone's house without invitation but the hosts would always receive him with joy and listen to his sermons with pleasure. His spontaneous visits, however, were always aimed at benefiting these people. For example, as soon as he learned that there was dissension and conflict in a family he immediately went to them and tried to restore peace. As a peacemaker, when he by accident hurt someone's feelings, he would immediately admit his fault and apologize.

In order to improve his priest's work and to benefit the souls entrusted to him, Father John would take well thought-out precautions in accordance with a particular situation. So sometimes he would appear among the poor as a lay person concealing his holy orders under secular clothes. It made talking to poor people easier and he could learn about their needs and do everything in his power to help them. He was happy if nobody recognized him in this appearance. Helping the needy materially, John also learned about their feelings and thoughts and gave them proper advice.

The door of the house of kind John was always open to people. He would often provide beggars with food and talked to the poverty-stricken nourishing them materially and spiritually. Parting with these guests dear to his heart Father John would give everyone what he could. People of other classes would also ask him for help and not in vain. Had anyone lost his property in a fire, Father John would lend him money so that he could provide himself with basic things. Had anyone become a beggar because of illness or adversity, he would give him alms that were enough to live on for a short time. In times of bad harvests poor peasants would borrow from Father John wheat seeds to sow the fields with and various household things or even would receive food for their starving families. Compassionate Father John would spend most of his income in alms, being satisfied with the little that was left. Out of mercy he would often intercede with the state authorities whom he knew, for those who had been harmed unjustly, and his intersession was in most cases successful.

Soon the fame of Father John's God-pleasing feats spread among the inhabitants of the capital. Visitors from various places would come to his house. These visits, however, were burdensome to him and for some time he did not receive anybody, but he continued to help the poor through his servants.

Father John tried to avoid fame and sought seclusion, but "A city that is set on a hill cannot be hid" (Mathew 5:14). According to divine intent Father John was to be elevated to a higher state to serve God and the people. The news about his virtuous life reached Peter I. According to the Tsar's order Father John was first summoned to hold a service at the court church and then appointed as the confessor of the sovereign and members of the royal family. By his exemplary piety Father John deserved the favour of all persons of high standing. Enjoying the Tsar's favour, Father John had even more possibilities to follow the merciful inclinations of his heart and be a generous father for orphans, a generous giver for the needy, an eager consoler of the sad, a prompt helper and intercessor for all who were miserable.

Father John was especially compassionate towards those who were imprisoned for crimes and debts. When visiting them, in order to conceal himself, he would leave his carriage before reaching the prison and would walk there. Having come to the prisoners he would greet them with fatherly love, sit next to them and ask them about the reason of their imprisonment with the greatest sympathy; it enabled him to understand everyone and to console them with the hope of God. Parting from them Father John would give them as many alms as he could. He would often give money to those who were imprisoned for debts so that they could pay them off. Visiting prisoners at Easter, at Christmas and during meat-fare week, he would kiss everyone with the usual Christian greeting and treat them to food that he had brought with him. When rumours spread about his feats, he began to visit prisons at night. But when he heard talking in the town about him, unfavourable and suspicious opinions, he decided to stop visiting prisons but continued to bestow charity through honest and conscientious people.

Thus Father John again secluded himself in his house with the intention to devote the rest of his life to praying. Except for church services he would not go anywhere and would not receive anybody even relatives and friends. Those who needed Father John's advice or instruction were to write to him and he would answer also in writing: he never refused such correspondence. Working and doing Christian feats, Father John reached old age unperceived and smoothly. Once he felt unwell and then he began to faint and have fits. He became so weak that he took to his bed and lay motionless. But the Lord who had given him this illness soon gave him back his health seeing his placid patience. This illness was a kind of presage of another misfortune and another disaster which were to befall the pious elder.

Upon recovery the elder ceased his seclusion and began to receive every visitor whoever he was. There were again a great number of visitors and Father John spent days and nights talking to them and teaching them the fear of God and piety. Parting with visitors he bade them farewell with a particular sadness as if having no hope of seeing them again. In fact the time had suddenly come for an ordeal for John, who was old already. Enemies accused the elder, who was not only absolutely guiltless but also noted for his high Christian virtues, of having dealings with the thief Grishka Talitsky and reported it to Peter I. The Tsar believed this mendacious denunciation, became angry and ordered to send the sixty-year old elder to archbishop Athanasios of Cholmogory, to be tonsured in the Solovetsky Monastery. Father John accepted this order as divine intent and went willingly to Cholmogory. On

March 13th 1701 he arrived at the archbishop's with the Tsar's edict. The kind archbishop received Father John as a brother and sent him on to the Solovetsky Monastery with an order from himself to tonsure John and to place him in obedience with an experienced elder. With meekness and trust in the divine will Father John appeared before the Superior of the cloister, archimandrite Firs who agreed to tonsure him according to the Tsar's will. "Christ God has led me to your holiness ordering me to be saved by you; and so I will do whatever you order me, unworthy one", said Father John. "Blessed be God who inspires you to feats; here is the place of salvation for you", said the archimandrite. The elder again made a low bow before the archimandrite asking him to honour him with the tonsure. On April 3rd the humble elder was tonsured by archimandrite Firs in the Cathedral, receiving the name of Job, which was reported to the Tsar.

The newly-tonsured monk was entrusted to the elder monk Jonah. Following devotedly his elder's will Father Job began to work to the best of his ability with a great desire to please the Lord God in everything, and he astonished all the brethren by his fasting, night vigil, submission and humility. The monk who shared a cell with Job said that this servant of Christ did not eat anything except bread and water, and the brethren called Father Job a fasting monk. First Father Job was assigned to do his work of obedience in the monastery kitchen. He worked zealously; he would arrive earlier than the others; he would chop wood and carry it on his old shoulders up the high stairs to the kitchen. He did other kinds of hard work with the same diligence. After the kitchen where he had worked hard he was assigned to another kind of obedience namely in the refectory. He performed this work with the same diligence and humility.

But the first enemy of man, wishing to destroy human souls, sees the feats of God's chosen ones and does his best to distract them from the path of salvation. So while Father Job was doing his work of obedience, the hater of all good, the tempter, would appear to him in the form of the monastery doctor and would say as if with compassion: "O my beloved friend! You should take care of your health, not to become feeble because of the yoke you have taken up for the sake of Christ, exhausting your body by work and fasting. God does not want work or fasting which is too much for someone to bear, but He seeks the pure and humble heart. You are old but you serve riassophore monks like a paid servant though you are not used to such work. Besides, you should not work in this manner because you are a priest-monk. It is enough that you have refused fame and honour in the world and have come here and work hard to earn your living. I am even surprised to see that you can eat this rough food after your past good food. Take care not to fall badly ill, then I will not be able to help you and you will die untimely. I will be so sorry if you do not follow my advice". "It is good not to spare the body so that it won't become stronger", answered Father Job to his pretended acquaintance, "however, even if the body becomes exhausted, God's power will still be realized through it. The Apostle said: "My grace is sufficient for thee: for my strength is made perfect in weakness. " Fasting is the mother of chastity – you eat with those who are like you". Having heard this answer the enemy immediately disappeared.

In these feats Father Job's spirit was becoming more and more attached to monasticism. In his enthusiasm for an ascetic life, he remembered the words of the Apostle: "No man that warreth entangleth himself with the affairs of this life; that he may please him who hath chosen him to be a soldier" (Timothy II 2:4), and distributed all he owned among beggars and the brethren of the monastery so that he could serve Christ without any hindrances. Having tested Father Job in obedience work the Superior of the monastery and all the brethren unanimously recognized him as a blameless monk, freed him from the work of obedience and allowed him to stay alone in a cell and work for his salvation. Keeping silence in his cell, Father Job would do the Jesus Prayer continuously, read the Holy Gospel, the Books of the Apostles, the Psalter, the vita of the venerated Zosima and Sabbatios and do needle-work. He would have a small portion of an ordinary brother's meals and did not cook anything for himself.

The fame of the ascetic of the Solovetsky Monastery spread all over the country and reached the Tsar. Peter I, having been convinced of the false accusation of his former confessor, wanted to bring him back to court, but Job asked the Tsar to allow him to stay on Solovki. His request was granted and after that he wished to live even more secluded than before. In 1702 with the blessing of archimandrite Firs he moved to the Anzer Hermitage.

In the hermitage the elder continued his monastic feats with even more zeal. Considering himself just a novice among the brethren of the hermitage he served everyone, especially the sick. At the same time he never missed church services and did his cell prayer rule.

Soon after Job's arrival at the hermitage, the head of the hermitage died. Knowing the pious and ascetic life of Father Job, archbishop Barnabas of Cholmogory suggested that archimandrite Firs honour the priest-monk Job with the position of head of the Anzer Hermitage. Job was summoned to the Solovetsky Monastery and having learnt the archbishop's will, accepted this appointment out of obedience. After that he asked the Superior to honour him with the tonsure of schemamonk but was refused. Upon receiving the Superior's blessing to assume the position of superior, he returned to the hermitage. Soon archimandrite Firs again summoned Father Job with some of the hermitage brethren to the monastery. Giving his final blessing for the appointment, the archimandrite told the new superior of the hermitage: "I entrust you the Anzer Hermitage dedicated to the Holy Trinity, take care of it, do not change its rule but follow the rule established by the holy fathers". The elder, having bid farewell to the archimandrite and the elders of the monastery, went to the hermitage. There he summoned all the brethren and performed first the thanksgiving prayer to the Holy Trinity with prostrations, then to the venerable Eleazar, the founder and protector of the hermitage. After that he greeted the brethren and he gave the following sermon: "I beseech you, my beloved brethren, to work to inherit the Kingdom of Heaven by fasting and praying. Let us take care of the salvation of our souls and abandon the evil path, that is fornication, theft, slander, idle talk, quarrels, hard drinking, gluttony and hatred of one's brother, let us avoid and disdain this, brethren, so as not to defile our souls, but let us follow the Lord's path leading us to the Kingdom of Heaven. Let us seek God in tears, fasting, vigil, submission to His will and obedience, and may we obtain the Lord's grace. Let us hate the world of illusion and remember the Lord's words: "If any man come to me, and hate not his father, and mother, and wife, and children, and brethren, and sisters, yea, and his own life also, he cannot be my disciple" (Luke 14:26)". We have renounced the world, brethren, so let us renounce all its evil affairs. The Lord says: "No man, having put his hand to the plough, and looking back, is fit for the kingdom of God" (Luke 9:62). How can we avoid eternal suffering if we lead our life in laziness? We, who have become monks, brethren, are to mourn and repent our sins. Repentance is the path leading to the Kingdom of Heaven; repentance is the key to the Kingdom of Heaven, without it nobody can enter it. Let us establish ourselves firmly on the path to the Kingdom of Heaven; the evil cannot approach it. This path may be sorrowful now, but then we will be joyful". The hermits listened to this sermon, bowed before Father Job and went to their cells.

In this new field of service Father Job, remembering the Lord's words: "For unto whomsoever much is given, of him shall much be required" (Luke 12:48), intensified his work and feats. He would constantly say the Jesus Prayer and work physically; he was the first to arrive in church and for obedience work and was the last to leave.

Job wanted to preserve the memory of the founder and of all ascetics of the Anzer Hermitage. It is known that the first writer of Eleazar's vita was Macarios, Job's associate. Macarios described Job in the book of the Anzer Hermitage as a wonderful man, "who abided in his earthly body like a bodiless angel". He also wrote that "Job was filled with the fear of God and the Holy Spirit" and in him there grew the wish to collect and write the lives of all the monks who were commemorated during the proscomidy (during Liturgy). He also tried to find out who were all the people who had given the church utensils. He had their names written down also and prayers were said for the well-being of those living and for the rest of the soul of the departed ones.

The number of brethren in the hermitage began to increase and soon there were thirty people there. The regulations of the hermitage were as follows: any candidate was to be accepted whether he was poor or rich but he was only to be warned about the difficulty of monastic feats. The novice was to wear his own clothes until he was used to the monastic life. After having allowed the novice to wear a cassock he would continue to be tested in various kinds of obedience; then when he became worthy he was tonsured a riassophore and the most praiseworthy were tonsured a schema-monk. Father Job taught everyone, especially newly-tonsured monks to humbly obey God and the authorities, saying that there was no salvation without obedience and that obedience was the main virtue. Besides the church and cell prayer rule, the hermits did physical work. At night the elder would inspect all the cells reminding the brethren of the night vigil. If he heard anyone praying he joyfully would move on, if he caught anyone talking he would knock on the door and move away upset; in the morning he would summon this brother and condemn him in private. He himself would pray all night kneeling, sometimes until the ringing of the bell and he was the first to come to the morning doxology.

According to Father Job the external behaviour of the monk should be as follows: to walk with the hands crossed on the chest; when meeting each other to bow with an affectionate look and with a friendly expression in the eyes; to love each other sincerely and to obey each other absolutely; to begin work always with the senior's permission and having made a mistake out of negligence to apologize and to try to reform.

The hermits who wanted to conduct an even more secluded life, with Father Job's blessing, lived in solitary cells. The elder supervised them and often visited them, inspiring them to eremitic feats and assigning them some needle-work. Being astute he sometimes exposed their sins before they repented of them.

Once Father Job remembered that our Lord Jesus Christ had told His disciples after having washed their feet: "For I have given you an example, that ye should do as I have done to you" (John 13:15) and began to reproach himself with tears : "Cursed are you! You have such a high position, you are a priest-monk and the head of the hermitage but you are not as humble as Christ the Saviour". After that he began to visit the sick and serve them, washing them and dressing their wounds; he would also put some anointing oil on some parts of their body and often healed them. He kept doing this feat of love and cared for his brothers until his death.

In 1710 the elder Job was summoned by the Superior of the Solovetsky Monastery, archimandrite Firs, and for his strict ascetic life he was honoured by being tonsured a schema-monk with the name Jesus in honor of Jesus (Joshua), the son of Nun, the Israelite leader who succeeded Moses.

The hieroschemamonk Jesus would often seclude himself and also would often go to hermits to have spiritual conversations with them, charging his disciples, the schemamonk Mathew and the monk Macarios, to take care of the hermitage while he was away. So on June 18th, the elder wanted to visit a hermit whom he respected very much, hierodeacon Paissios who lived 21000 feet from the hermitage by the high mountain which is now called Golgotha and which is noted for the fact that the venerable Eleazar stayed on it. After the conversation the elder expressed his wish to stay with the hermit for a while and Father Paissios gave him a separate cell.

Once, Jesus as usual began to do the evening prayer and did it till midnight reading psalms and remaining on his knees. Having become tired he sat down and in a dream he saw an unusual light in his cell and the Most Holy Mother of God in the radiance of heavenly glory accompanied by the venerable

Eleazar of Anzer. In devout fear he stood up and made a prostration before them. While doing this he heard the voice of the Heavenly Queen: "Henceforth this mountain will be called the second Golgotha; a great stone church dedicated to the Crucifixion of My Son the Lord will be built on it, and a new hermitage will be organised for you and your two disciples, the schemamonk Mathew and the monk Macarios, the hermitage will receive the name of Crucifixion, and many monks will come to you and God's name will be glorified. I will personally visit the mountain and will be with you forever". With these words the vision finished and the elder heard another voice from above: "Consecrate the mountain Golgotha and put a cross on it!" The pious elder was greatly surprised with what he had heard and seen and told the hierodeacon Paissios about it. Paissios carved all he had heard from Jesus on the cross made by the elder.

On June 29th, the feast of the Apostles Peter and Paul, hieroschemamonk Jesus fulfilling God's will left the Anzer Hermitage with his disciples Macarios and Mathew for the mountain Golgotha; there he sprinkled the mountain with holy water, erected the cross with the writing on it and then built a prayer hut for the all-night night vigil. Upon consecrating the mountain and erecting the cross the hermits prostrated themselves and performed the thanksgiving prayer to the Lord God and the Most Holy Mother of God. Since then the elder began to organize a new hermitage on the mountain Golgotha. In 1713 he went with his disciple Macarios to archbishop Barnabas of Cholmogory to ask for his blessing to build a church and a hermitage on the mountain Golgotha. The archbishop by the edict of July 15th 1713, approved the construction of two stone churches, one on the mountain Golgotha dedicated to the Crucifixion of the Lord, the other at the foot of the mountain, on the place of the appearance of the Most Holy Mother of God, dedicated to Her Dormition. The same edict approved the organization of a hermitage and gave it the name of the Crucifixion and the mountain the name of Golgotha. First the blessed elder was happy about the archbishop's order, but then having encountered various difficulties and deficiencies in the construction of stone churches he had to ask the archbishop to allow a wooden church with a refectory to be built at the top of the mountain instead of the two stone churches. Archbishop Barnabas by the edict of September 18th 1714, approved the construction of a small wooden church on the mountain dedicated to the Beheading of the Prophet, Forerunner and Baptist John.

Upon receiving this last written edict the elder left the Anzer Hermitage and with several disciples moved to the mountain Golgotha. Having settled on its top he began to organize a hermitage. Soon Jesus' disciples built a wooden church which was consecrated by archimandrite Firs in honour of the Crucifixion of the Lord according to the edict of the archbishop of May 15th 1715.

When Peter I learned about the appearance of the Most Holy Mother of God to the blessed elder and the newly-built hermitage dedicated to the Crucifixion on Golgotha, he helped him generously, out of special favour to his former confessor. So soon an edict was issued to deliver annually bread from the state bakery of Arkhangelsk to the brethren of the Golgotha Hermitage. In 1714, at the beginning of the construction of the hermitage the Tsaritsa Maria Alekseevna donated to the church of Golgotha many precious things, clothes and books inscribed "For the Golgotha Hermitage". The most precious donation was the local holy icon of the Dormition of the Mother of God with silver plating and gilding and with an attached box filled with holy relics. The Tsarina Parasceve Fyodorovna (widow of Tsar Ivan Alekseevich) in addition to other donations granted 100 rubles for the church's construction on the mountain Golgotha and prince Menshikov gave 100 gold coins. There were also many other donors. But it was Tsaritsa Maria Alekseevna who took special care of the construction of the Golgotha-Crucifixion Hermitage. Here is her letter on this subject to archimandrite Thyrsos:

"May God's grace, peace and love as well as constant welfare be granted to the archimandrite of the cloister of the Wonder-workers of Solovki and the brethren. This letter is first of all written to ask you to take care of all supplies, including bricks, of the Holy Crucifixion Hermitage of Anzer intended for the construction of the stone church of the Crucifixion of the Lord. Thus we ask you to care for this God-chosen and blessed place and for bricks in particular. Though now there is an impediment to this construction due to the replacement of the vice-governor Alexis Kurbatov, may the all-gracious Lord bless those who fear Him and may He hear their prayers and send churchwardens to this church. Right Reverend Archimandrite, order to make bricks in advance and take money for all kinds of supplies from Father Jesus. Let us repeat: we ask and order to take proper care of these needs and the all-gracious Lord will reward you. And we will be obliged to you. We rely on your holy prayers. Tsarevna Maria from the ruling city of Moscow, March 15th 1715".

In 1718 the newly-built hermitage was attacked by robbers, they beat the brethren mercilessly, chased them away and took the church and hermitage belongings and these were not found afterwards. At this time of sorrow the blessed elder stayed constantly in his cell and prayed to the Lord God to save the brethren. The hermits, who had run away, came back to the hermitage to their spiritual father. The elder reproached them for their cowardice and the monks promised in future to die rather than leave the hermitage whatever might happen.

The hermitage began to grow as many people were coming to lead an ascetic life under the guidance of the wise teacher. Nobody was refused; everyone was accepted with love. There was only one condition: anyone who wanted to join the hermitage was to build a cell for himself, though sometimes the elder would help him. Soon there were twenty brethren besides the hermits who lived in secluded places under the supervision of Father Jesus and who would come to the hermitage every Sunday to attend the divine service and confess to the elder. All these ascetics led a life of spiritual feats and physical work. To give an example to others the old head of the hermitage himself would sometimes chop wood, carry water up the mountain to the kitchen and make dough for bread in the bakery. Once on the feast of the Dormition of the Mother of God the cellarer of the hermitage came to the elder and said: "Father, there is nobody to bring water to the kitchen". The elder stood up and began to carry water from the lake to the top of the mountain, but when the brethren saw the elder doing it, they ran out of their cells and brought plenty of water. Sometime later the cellarer came again to the blessed elder and complained: "Order, father, one of the brethren who is not busy now to chop wood for the kitchen". "I am not busy", replied the blessed elder, "So I will go and chop wood". It was dinner time. The elder blessed the brethren to have dinner, then took an axe and began to chop wood. After dinner the brethren also began to chop wood for their own use. In his spare time the blessed elder Jesus always did needle-work. If it happened that he earned some money he divided it into three parts: one for the church needs, the second for the brethren's needs, the third for alms for beggars. The elder did not have any money saved, he did not possess any property either except for some ecclesiastical books. As far as clothes were concerned he was satisfied to have only two robes, one made of horsehair which was coarse and which he wore next to the skin and the other which was even worse and which he wore over the first one. The elder did not pay any attention to reproaches about such a simple way of life. He also had the habit of going to any brother who was ill and serving him till he recovered.

But who can list all the spiritual feats of the blessed elder? They are known only to God for whom they were done. As before, Jesus never missed the church services and was the first to arrive; and he would spend all night making prostrations and doing his cell prayer rule. During Great Lent he would shut himself in his cell and spend the whole of Lent in seclusion in permanent prayer. He would leave this seclusion only before the very holy feast of Easter.

The venerated Jesus made the hermitage rules for his disciples and this was the most notable part : "If someone wants to live in the hermitage with me or after me he should not eat the following food: beef, milk and fish; and he should not drink wine. The common meal should consist of vegetables with a little sunflower-seed oil. He should not have personal objects in his cell, meet women nor have any boys to do obedience work for him... Besides the church rule he should do five kathismas from the Psalter, 500 Jesus Prayers and 300 prostrations".

For his God-pleasing life the elder was honoured with special revelations. Some of his disciples complained of the difficulty of carrying water to

the top of the mountain from the lake which was a
kilometre away from the hermitage. Then the elder
began to pray in the evening and prayed assiduously
till midnight. In his prayer he asked the Lord
God and the Most Holy Mother of God to help the
brethren. At midnight he went into ecstasy and saw
an ineffable light in the cell: the Most Holy Mother of
God appeared to him in the radiance of her heavenly
glory with the venerated Eleazar of Anzer and
two Angels. The elder fell to the ground before the
Mother of God. She told him: "Stand up! Your prayer
has been heard; tomorrow take your disciples and
dig a well on the mountain (and She showed the
place); here you will find water for yourself and the
brethren". After She had disappeared the blessed
elder told his disciples about his vision. In the
morning they went to the indicated place, began to
dig a well and reached an abundant source of water.
Everyone accepted this event as a sign of the Divine
care for the hermitage and rejoiced, glorifying God
and the Most Holy Mother of God by the hymn:
"Wonderful are Your works, Lord…" When the well
was made the elder and the brethren celebrated
divine liturgy and thanksgiving prayers to God with
prostrations, then they went in procession to the
new spring. After consecrating the water in the well
the elder sprinkled this water in the church, the
brethren's cells and the top of the mountain, singing
the hymn to the Holy Spirit: "The grace of the Holy
Spirit gathered us today…" After completing the
rite the elder preached a sermon to his disciples.
He said: "Do not grieve, brethren, do not lose heart,
but always trust in God. By His almighty word the
Lord brought sweet water from the earth's interior
for all who live on the earth, both faithful and
unfaithful; how could He abandon us, His servants,
and not nourish us? Let us remember His promise:

"A mother is more likely to forget her children than I am likely to forget you!"

Once at night robbers came to the elder to rob him, they did not know that he had nothing to steal. Having hidden in the cell they were waiting for the elder to go to church for the morning service. The elder was not sleeping, he was doing his prayer rule and heard them coming, or rather foresaw their intention. So he added to his prayer : "God, give sleep to Your servants who have become tired pleasing the enemy". The prayer was heard and the unwanted visitors fell asleep and slept in the elder's cell for five days and five nights until the elder came with the brethren and woke them with the words: "How long are you going to lie in wait for nothing? Go home". They got up, but could not walk because they had stayed without food for a long time. The elder fed them and let them go. Afterwards he learned that these people had been called to account for this deed and sent a petition to deliver them from the trial. Meanwhile he sold all the books he had and gave the money to beggars fearing that someone else might get into the same trouble. After having been released the wrongdoers came to the Golgotha Hermitage, asked the elder forgiveness and his blessing and worked for the brethren all summer.

Once robbers came to the elder's vegetable garden. They filled their bags with vegetables, put them on their shoulders but could not move and stood there for two days and two nights motionless. Then they began to cry: "Holy Father, let us go". Some of the brethren heard them crying and came to them but could not move them. The monks asked them: "When did you come here?" "We have been standing here for two days and two nights". "We have been coming here all the time. Why didn't we see you?" "We didn't see you either, if we had seen you we would have asked your elder forgiveness".

The elder came and told the robbers: "You have been idle and you have stolen the fruit of other people's work, so stand here idly for the rest of your life". The robbers pleaded with tears to let them go, promising not to do anything like this in future. The elder said: "If you want to work with your own hands and to feed others with the fruit of your work then I will let you go". They vowed to follow his order. Then he said: "Blessed be God strengthening you: work for the brethren in this cloister for a year ". After that he freed them from the invisible ties by his prayer and they stayed and worked in the hermitage.

One of the hermitage brethren suffered from the temptation of fornication. He came to the Saint to ask for help and was ready to do whatever the elder would order. The elder talked about living in continence, touched the brother's body with his staff and the carnal passion immediately disappeared. After that the monk never again suffered from it.

Years passed and the elder who had labored so much and who had experienced so many vicissitudes in his life was approaching the end of his days on earth. The lamp of life had begun to burn low in him and he became very weak. The Saint started to prepare for the transition to eternal life. He now concentrated on himself though without ceasing to care for his brothers. He would often sing to himself with tears: "My soul, my soul, arise! Why are you sleeping? The end is drawing near, and you will be confounded". The elder would also often go to the grave that he had made with his own hands and would shed tears and sigh, contemplating death and divine justice.

The Lord not only revealed to His faithful servant his approaching death but even the very day it would happen. The blessed elder told the brethren in advance that he would die on Sunday before sunrise. Being ill and bedridden the elder called his disciples and among other things told them: "I am leaving you for the eternal life; you must stay in the hermitage and continue your service for which you are predestined by God".

But soon the elder's illness was aggravated by a bad fever. Being totally exhausted with it he only kept repeating to himself: "May the Lord's will be done, may the Lord do whatever He wishes" and then he would sink in prayer. The dying ascetic lay motionless for three days and nights and his breath was hardly noticeable, so the brethren cried expecting his death. But to their general joy and surprise, after three days, the elder suddenly felt better, got up and addressed the brethren with the words: "The time of my life is over as the Lord informed me! Choose among yourselves a teacher and I will bless him". After a day the elder blessed his senior disciple Macarios, chosen by the brethren as his successor and entrusted them to him. Macarios made a low bow before his dying father and promised to follow all his precepts.

Feeling better, hieroschemamonk Jesus celebrated the Divine Liturgy for the last time and administered the Lord's Sacrament to all his disciples. After the liturgy he felt exhausted and went to bed and never got up again. During his last minutes he was filled with unusual joy which proved that he was ready to enter eternity. Even on his deathbed the blessed elder continued caring for the construction of a stone church in the hermitage. In 1719 he had entreated the head of the Anzer Hermitage, Herman, to store a good sum of money for bricks and other materials. But these preparations stopped because Herman was transferred to another monastery. On his deathbed Jesus asked the new superior of the Anzer Hermitage, Spiridon, to continue the construction of the church and gave him 236 roubles. It was enough for the construction. Being near death he also gave hieromonk Philaret, the monk Proclos and the novice Onesime 100 gold coins and 38 roubles for this construction. Jesus lived until Sunday which was the first day of the Great Lent. Early in the morning he called all his disciples, kissed them for the last time and blessed each one of them, and the disciples showed their devotion to the elder by crying bitterly. Having bid farewell to everyone hieroschemamonk Jesus said: "I am going to my Lord Jesus Christ and now father Macarios will be your guide to the Kingdom of Heaven; follow him on the path of virtue. I also ask you not to wash my body after death, not to change my clothes, but to put me in the coffin with the clothes I am wearing now. Bury me on your own without the help of lay people". When the crying monks asked: "Holy Father, how can we live without you? We would like to die with you, for you have been leading us to Christ and now you are leaving us", the elder said: "Do not worry, my beloved brethren, for I am parting with you only in body, but I will always be with you in spirit". Having said these words he let them go to their cells. One of the disciples who had served the elder while he had been ill, left him, but did not go to his cell. Instead he began to watch the elder secretly through the keyhole and saw him get up, kneel in the middle of the cell and pray with tears to God and the Most Holy Mother of God, calling also upon the saints, and often mentioning in his prayer the hermitage he had built, and the brethren. After the prayer he lay on the bed and crossed himself. Some minutes later he again got up and prayed to the Lord on his knees with raised hands: "O Lord my God! I thank You for having accepted my humility and letting me die in the Orthodox Christian faith in You, in keeping and fulfilling Your commandments! Accept, O Lord, my spirit in peace, and preserve Your servants

whom You gathered through me in one flock..."
This prayer of the virtuous ascetic was not long and soon he lay on the bed again. At this moment his face changed: with eyes turned to the sky his face began to shine with an inexplicable calmness and joy. He was motionless and silent and as if speaking with someone within his soul. Suddenly the elder interrupted his silence with the exclamation: "Blessed be the God of our fathers! If so I am no longer afraid but leave this world joyfully!" With these words an unusual light and a great fragrance appeared in the cell, and the sweetest voice began singing the psalm: "I had gone with the multitude, I went with them to the house of God, with the voice of joy and praise, with a multitude that kept holyday" (Psalm 42:4)" At this moment the blessed one turned his face upwards, stretched his legs, put his hands crosswise on his chest, and his soul flew to heaven where it had always longed to arrive during its earthly journey.

"Precious in the sight of the Lord is the death of his saints" (Psalm 115:16). This word of the Lord was realized in the case of hieroschemamonk Jesus whom the Lord allowed to pass away in old age, peacefully and quietly, after pious deeds, on the first Sunday of Great Lent, in the morning, before the sunrise, on March 6th 1720, as the elder had predicted a long time before his death.

Having come back to their cells the disciples suddenly heard beautiful prayerful singing, and thinking that the morning service had already started, hurried to the church, but to their great surprise they found it closed. Bewildered they listened attentively to the singing: it seemed to be coming from the dying elder's cell. They all hurried there and found the Saint having already peacefully given his soul to the Lord. The disciples began to cry bitterly; they lamented parting from their father and not seeing him dying. Having put the ascetic's body in the coffin they left it in the cell.

The disciples did not divulge the blessed elder's death but the monks of the Solovetsky Monastery and the Anzer Hermitage learnt about it and soon the Golgotha Hermitage was filled with visitors bringing incense, wax candles, oil and other things. Everybody wanted their offerings to be used during the burial. The monks and lay people who had come to the hermitage surrounded the cell waiting for the elder's body to be buried, but few of them were able to witness it. Heavy rain forced the people to leave and the disciples took advantage of the opportunity and fulfilled the elder's commandment by burying him without any lay people. The burial service took place in the church three days after his death, that is on Wednesday, the second week of Great Lent, after the Liturgy of the Presanctified. The service was celebrated by hieromonks Hyacinth, Philaret and Proclos, and hierodeacons in the presence of all the brethren of the hermitage and of hermits who came to pay their respects to their father. When the last thing to be done was to kiss the deceased elder, his will concerning the brethren was found sealed in an envelope and read aloud. In this will the Saint first praised the Lord God for all His goodness to him during his long life, then he consoled the disciples, bade them farewell, thanked all benefactors who were still alive and finally announced that he had no possessions. The monks of the hermitage themselves carried the body of the elder, and put it into a stone vault made on the mountain at a depth of 0,7 m. Over the vault they put a well-made wooden tomb with an inscription and they also put a wooden board on the tomb with the following words: "Here, on March 6th 1720, died the venerable Job (in the schema named Jesus), first, superior of the Anzer Hermitage and then of the Golgotha Hermitage.

Born in 1635. He became a monk in 1701. He came to the Anzer Hermitage to live in seclusion in 1702. He became the superior of the Anzer Hermitage in 1706. He was tonsured a schemamonk in 1710. He came to the mountain Golgotha and became the superior of the Golgotha Hermitage in 1714. He was an example of virtue by his word and his life, by love and spirit, by faith and the purity of his heart. He lived for 85 years. On March 9th 1720, he was buried here". From the day of the burial the brethren began to hold services for the dead and after a while the disciples of the blessed elder put a chapel over the tomb and painted the face of the Saint on the tomb board.

After the death of the blessed elder matters concerning the Golgotha-Crucifixion Hermitage changed their course. The superior of the Anzer Hermitage announced that the late elder allegedly had ordered his spiritual father to give both the money and materials he had prepared, to the Anzer Hermitage to build a warm side-chapel devoted to the Birth of the Most Holy Mother of God. The money was used according to the head's will but the church that was built in the Anzer Hermitage soon burned down with its sacristy and all the church property. Being unable to find any protection the elder's disciples had to go to the Solovetsky Monastery and the Anzer Hermitage. Only two hermits stayed on the mountain Golgotha – the monks Gennadios and Serge. The authorities of the Solovetsky Monastery took all the hermitage and church property from them and gave it to the Anzer Hermitage. Finally, by the decree of the Holy Synod of July 23rd 1723 (Number 496), the Golgotha-Crucifixion Hermitage was united with the Anzer Trinity Hermitage because there were few monks left in the Golgotha-Crucifixion Hermitage.

But the mountain Golgotha, the holy place, made famous by the appearance of the Most Holy Mother of God, did not remain deserted. The monks seeking seclusion, alone, by twos or by threes or even more, continued to live in the former hermitage.

In 1764, when the "Ecclesiastical classification" was introduced, the Golgotha-Crucifixion Hermitage was attached to the Solovetsky Monastery and since then the superiors of the Solovetsky Monastery began to manage it. In 1768, according to the decree of the Holy Synod, all precious things that had been removed from the Golgotha-Crucifixion Hermitage and stored in Arkhangelsk, in the bishop's house - mostly gifts of former royalty: Gospels, chalices, censers, vestments and other things – were returned to the Golgotha-Crucifixion Hermitage.

Until 1826 the monks from the Solovetsky Monastery who sought silence and seclusion lived in the Golgotha-Crucifixion Hermitage. The wooden church built by Jesus had become dilapidated. But in 1826 the hermitage was restored by the superior of the Solovetsky Monastery, archimandrite Dositheos. By order of the Holy Synod a new stone church devoted to the Crucifixion of the Lord Jesus Christ and a warm side-chapel devoted to the Dormition of the Most Holy Mother of God were built and consecrated in the Golgotha Hermitage on September 13th 1830. The tomb of the blessed elder hieroschemamonk Jesus, is situated on the left side of this side-chapel. The wooden church built by the elder was transferred to the foot of the mountain, to the place where the Most Holy Mother of God had appeared to the blessed elder for the first time, that is, to the place where the cell of the hermit hierodeacon Paisios had been situated. Since that time a hieromonk from the brethren of the Solovetsky Monastery, experienced in the monastic life, has been regularly appointed superior, and ten or more monks have been appointed to be under his charge; the latter are chosen from those who are particularly inclined to an ascetic and silent life and long for it.

The regulations of the hermitage established by the founder, the elder Jesus, concerning the church and cell prayer rule and fasting have been followed precisely except that because of the weakness of the brethren the new superior of the hermitage, archimandrite Dositheos, allowed them to have fish on the days sanctioned by the church.

In the Golgotha-Crucifixion Hermitage, in the warm side-chapel devoted to the Dormition of the Most Holy Mother of God, by the tomb of the founder, the psalter is read uninterruptedly day and night except when a divine service is celebrated in this church. The rest of the time, every two hours three chimes of the bell are heard, which means that the monk-reader is changed. The purpose of this reading is to glorify continuously the name of God and to commemorate both living and dead benefactors. So with every psalm a prayer is offered for the health of the most pious tsar of Russia and his august family, the Holy Synod, all the brethren of the Solovetsky Monastery, the brethren of the hermitage, benefactors and visitors of the cloister and all Orthodox Christians. This prayer is followed by the prayer for the dead – for their eternal peace in the hope of the resurrection according to the faith in the risen Lord.

In summer, thousands of pilgrims come from the Solovetsky Monastery to Golgotha in spite of the inevitable danger of sailing across a rough sea to the Anzersky Island. It is moving to see these pilgrims kneeling with reverence before the tomb of the blessed elder and zealously serving the Office of the Dead for the repose of the soul of this great elder adding the names of their deceased relatives and friends.

The monks who lived in the time of the saintly elder describe his appearance in the following way: he was of medium height and a good build; he had a broad smooth face with reddish cheeks. His eyes were light and penetrating, his look was pleasant; his hair was white, curly and spread beautifully on his shoulders; his nose and mouth were medium; his beard was thick and as white as his hair; it was three palms long and forked at the end.

Hermit Theophane

We have been speaking about the monks of the Solovetsky Island who lived a long time ago and who are remembered today. But the place hallowed by the virtues and feats of Saints Zosima and Sabbatios and their zealous followers, in our time also had true servants of God who strove for their salvation and steadily followed the path of their fathers. It would not be true to say that our time is not appropriate to pleasing God and that there are no more true ascetics like the ancient saints. Time is not an insuperable hindrance to those who sincerely long for salvation: salvation depends on our own will and determination; God's grace which strengthened the ancient ascetics is the same now; it is inexhaustible for people and as permanent as God Himself. In order on the one hand, to prove that there are now also people who please God, and on the other hand, to give an example to those seeking salvation we will tell the story of the ascetics of our century who led and finished their earthly life doing feats of Christian piety.

Origin. – Novitiate. – Journey to Moldavia. – Life in the Nyamets Monastery. – Return to Kiev. – Dositheos. – Arrival at the Solovetsky Monastery. – Seclusion. – Return to the monastery. – Life in Sumy. – Working as a manager of the household. – The bell ringer's story. – Retreat to the Pomorsky sea shore. – Life in seclusion. – Return to the Solovetsky Monastery. – Life in the Golgotha-Crucifixion Hermitage. – Precepts. – Temptation. – Vision. – Illness. – Death

Theophane was Ukrainian by origin. His parents were farmers. When he was twelve years old he lost his parents and became an orphan with his small brother and sister. At sixteen Theophane began to do the farming. Once when he was working in the field, a divine light illuminated his soul and deep emotion filled his heart: he immediately unharnessed his oxen, left the field and the plough and without even saying goodbye to his brother and sister went away from his native land carried along by love for Christ. He came to the Kievo-Pecherskaya Lavra and was admitted as a novice. There he spent seventeen years doing various kinds of work and serving the ascetic Dositheos who had already lived in seclusion for thirty years. Dositheos never left his cell and did not receive anybody; those who wanted to receive a blessing and directions from him could speak to him through the window of his cell. His talent of speaking was combined with second sight : he exposed secret sins and stimulated to repentance; he warned against future troubles and temptations. It was noticed that when he gave a prosphora or a staff, it betokened recovery and welfare; when he gave incense, it betokened death. Theophane learned from this ascetic how to lead a monastic life. Soon he felt a longing to visit holy places marked by the events of the earthly life of the Lord Jesus Christ. When Theophane asked his elder the blessing to set out on a long journey he was given the following answer: "You are to go neither to Jerusalem nor to the Holy Mountain; you are predestined to make another journey; and now if you go to Moldavia, it will benefit you". He told Theophane to go to Podol (the lower part of the city of Kiev), to find there two Moldavian monks and to bring them to him.

The Hermit Theophane

One of these monks was Sophronios, a friend and associate of Paisios who later became an archimandrite. Having fulfilled all the errands given to him by Paisios, Sophronios was going to set out on his home journey, when Dositheos summoned him and asked him to take his disciple with him. The Moldavian monks took Theophane willingly with them and resorted to his services on the way. This journey seemed so hard to Theophane because of the oppressions of the Turks and various hardships that he regretted having left Kiev. Near the Nyamets monastery the travellers were met by Paisios who greeted Theophane with the following words: "Child Theophane! Your journey here was not in vain, it will bring you your reward". Theophane was kindly received and first stayed in the Nyamets Monastery and then visited other cloisters, looking at their locations, studying the monastic rules, customs and habits. He considered the example of these monks' lives very instructive. They were not acquisitive: there was nothing in their cells except icons, a book and instruments for their work. The monks were noted for their humility and absence of pride and vanity; they did not know hatred and resentment; if anyone out of carelessness or hot temper happened to offend another monk, he hurried to be reconciled with him. The monk who did not want to forgive the brother who had sinned was banished from of the monastery. The monks walked humbly and devoutly: with downcast eyes, bowing to each other when they met, in church each monk would stand on his own place, there was no idle talk, not only in church but also inside and outside the monastery. At that time about seven hundred brethren lived with elder Paisios and when a hundred or a hundred and fifty brethren would gather to do obedience work, one of them would read a book or tell a moral story. If anyone started idle talk, he was immediately stopped. In their cells some monks would write books, others would spin, still others would make skufias, kamilavkas, carve spoons, crosses or do other work. Everybody was under the supervision of spiritual fathers and teachers; no one would dare eat a piece of fruit without permission although there are plenty in this country; only with a blessing and all together would they eat the fruit of the earth to the glory of God.

Theophane liked this kind of life very much and asked Paisios to let him stay in Moldavia. "Now go to Russia", said Paisios, "and serve the elder who is going to die soon, follow his will and go and seek salvation in the place he will tell you". Blessing him at parting he added: "Child, may God and the Most Pure guard you on the way; I believe that God will not allow you to be tempted excessively and He will give honour to His chosen ones through the prayers of the holy Fathers Anthony and Theodose, the wonder-workers of the Kievo-Pecherskya Lavra, and your elder Dositheos; may you be given God's blessing through our humility. Thank your devout elder and do not forget our poverty". Theophane was supplied with whatever was necessary and arrived in Kiev safely. Dositheos spent his last years in seclusion in the Kitaevsky Hermitage. Having felt his approaching death, the hermit told his disciple: "My beloved child, you have served me well and for a long time; now I am returning to my fathers; when you bury me, do not stay here, but go to the north; there in the Solovetsky monastery you will find salvation". Theophane answered: "Father, I promised to spend my life by the caves of Saint Anthony and Theodose". "Child", said the elder, "Anthony and Theodose here are equal before God to Zosima and Sabbatios there; they have received the same grace from God to intercede for their spiritual children. I see that Divine Providence directs you to the north and I believe that it does everything which is good for you and for the salvation of your soul; it will help you to bear the hardships of seclusion. Do not oppose the will of the Highest, but staying there listen to yourself and guard yourself against the fierce beast trying to devour you. If you experience temptation do not despair but try to reform yourself with fortitude". These were the instructions that Dositheos gave his disciple before his death. After a thirty-year long seclusion he died in 1778 being 53 years old. Later it became known that the hermit Dositheos was the maiden Darya from the noble family of the Tyapins from Ryazan. From her second to her ninth year she lived in the cell of her grandmother, the nun Porphiria in the Voznesensky Monastery in Moscow. When Porfiria was tonsured to the schema, Darya was again taken to her house where she lived till the age of fifteen. When she left the monastery she was like a perfect nun: she would not eat anything on wednesdays and fridays; she would not have milk and eggs at all; she would avoid not only games but also any communication with people; finally, she went to a forest with her sisters as if to have a walk and escaped. Her parents sought her in vain. After three years Darya's sister and mother went to the Lavra of Saint Serge and there in a young monk lighting a candle she noticed a surprising resemblance with her lost sister. She asked some hieromonk to bring this monk to her. The hieromonk passed on the invitation, but the young monk had already left the monastery of St. Serge. After twelve years Darya's sister came to Kiev and spoke to the hermit Dositheos but he did not show his face and advised her not to seek relatives who might have run away for the sake of God. When the sister came to Kiev once again Dositheos had already died.

At first the monk Theophane did not follow his elder's order and stayed in Kiev. Having dug a cave, he was going to settle in it, but was not allowed to do so; then he wanted to live in seclusion near the Lavra but was forbidden. Seeing that he was not favoured by God because he disobeyed his elder, he left Kiev and went to the remote Solovetsky Monastery. He came to the cloister when its superior was archimandrite Hieronim and began to do various kinds of work of obedience beginning in the prosphora bakery. There he found the monk Clement who was leading an ascetic life. Clement would tell his body: "I am pacifying you by eating unboiled food, hunger and thirst so that you become obedient to me and do your work carrying the burden which was put on you". Sometimes Theophane and Clement talked about the hermits who had lived on the Solovetsky Island before and, being known to God only, had spent their lives in hunger and thirst eating only moss and various berries and experiencing various hardships, frost and the attacks of the enemies of salvation. But those ascetics overcame all difficulties with fortitude having armed themselves with faith and prayer. These talks aroused in Clement a wish to live in seclusion and he asked his elder a blessing to do so. Seeing his steadfast intention and knowing his patience the elder let him go. Just like a deer rushes to a source of water he rushed inland to desert places. There at the foot of a mountain he found a suitable place, dug a cave and began to live in fasting and prayer.

Theophane took care of his former workmate and sent him everything necessary. But soon his whereabouts were discovered by one of the monastery workers who informed archimandrite Hieronim about him. The archimandrite ordered to bring him back to the monastery prosphora bakery. But Clement found no peace being consumed with the wish to live in seclusion. In the spring he again received his elder's permission to retire. At first Theophane grieved losing him but then he secretly left the monastery and began to look for his friend Clement in the remotest places of the island. Having failed to find him, he made a mud-house near the lake Yagodnoye, ten km from the monastery, and settled in it. At night the hermit would sing the psalter and make prostrations and in the daytime he would work and gather moss and roots to eat. His old wish to live in seclusion was satisfied; in seclusion his soul felt at home. The devil would frighten Theophane with various visions: sometimes wild animals would appear to him or plenty of birds of prey would fly at him screetching; sometimes a mounted army of enemies would appear to him; sometimes he would even suffer a beating. Then he would pray God for help and intercession and the Lord would save him.

But Theophane still hoped to find Clement or other hermits somewhere; with that end in mind he would walk about the nearby mountains and valleys. Once he found two hermits who had lived together in one cell for seven years. He spent the night with them and learned about their prayer rule: they would rise at midnight, then one of them would make prostrations, while the other would pray with raised hands for himself and his brother; after that the first one would take his place, and the other brother would make prostrations. Another time while he was travelling around the island he met the people who had been sent to seek him; he returned with them to the monastery. Soon Theophane was sent to Sumy to supervise the farmstead of the Solovetsky Monastery. Life in the world changed Theophane's spiritual mood; he spent three years and a half in Sumy taking care of material things and then he was sent to Arkhangelsk to make some purchases. Hieronim's successor, archimandrite Gerasim, appointed Theophane manager of the housekeeping of the cloister. There the bell ringer once passed him greetings from his former workmate. "Is Clement still alive?" asked Theophane with some fear. "Yes, he is alive", answered the bell ringer and told him about meeting Clement. Having visited the Anzer Hermitage and the mountain

Golgotha, the bell ringer was coming back when he turned off the road to pick up some berries and lost his way; he wandered about the island for two days and then on the third day he saw smoke on the mountain. Having gone up the mountain he found a hole and then a door to a cell. With the usual prayer he entered the cell and saw a praying hermit, he bowed to him, sat down and at the invitation of the hermit told him about himself. Then the hermit recognized in the bell ringer his old acquaintance and said to him that he was Clement, Theophane's colleague in the prosphora bakery. When the bell ringer asked Clement how he had come there and how he had lived all this time, Clement told him:

"I left the monastery and went to the sea; there on the sea shore I found three logs, made a raft and set out to sea calling upon Jesus Christ: "Lord Jesus Christ, my God! You know my intention: wishing to serve only You, I avoid people. If You wish to save my soul on this island, keep me here; and if You have another place for me, lead me there. I beseech you, Lord, do not deprive me of Your Providence, but may Your will be done in everything". With this prayer I began to move away from the shore rowing with a piece of wood; there came a fair wind and soon I landed on the Anzerskry Island. Seeking a suitable place to live I came here, built a hut and since then I have been serving God in seclusion for six years". "What do you eat?" asked the bell ringer, "And are you attacked by evil spirits?" The hermit showed him some roots he made food of, and said that in the beginning he suffered much from evil spirits. Sometimes they would come in the form of fishers and drive him out, sometimes they would appear in the form of wild animals and rush to him being ready to tear him to pieces". "Tell me", asked the hermit, "whether father Theophane is alive and how he is". "He is alive and now he does the monastery purchases", answered the bell ringer. When Clement heard this, he struck his chest, fell to the ground and said crying: "Woe is me, the sinner! I hear what I did not want to; tell him, for God's sake, that he is perishing, tell him about my sorrow. Where is his previous ascetic life? Where is his longing for virtue and his wish to live in seclusion? Living in the world and facing its temptations, he is more and more stuck in worldly cares. Those three hermits whom the treasurer John had seen did their feats and died in peace with God; I buried them with my own hands".

The bell ringer spent all night talking to Clement and in the morning he asked the hermit for a blessing, learnt about the way to the hermitage and went back home.

The bell ringer's story struck Theophane very much. While his friend was serving God, he was occupied with worldly cares and did not have time to take care of his soul. Sorrow and repentance filled his heart and he began to seek a way to reform his life. Soon God revealed the way of repentance to him. The new archimandrite Gerasim striving to bring order to the cloister reprimanded Theophane who supervised the monastery work. Theophane decided to leave the Solovetsky Monastery; he took a small boat and some bread and set out to sea with the intention of settling on the Pomorsky sea shore. First the wind was gentle but then a storm began. Having a presentiment of death, Theophane cried: "Lord Jesus Christ, have mercy on me! You know I entrusted myself to these waves for Your sake. I appeal to Your mercy, give me time to repent, for I see that the waves are ready to devour me, may the abyss not bring to hell my soul which is not ready yet to stand before the last judgement". The waves were so strong that it was impossible to sail or to row. Theophane lay down in the middle of the boat expecting death to come any minute. So he was carried by the sea for ten days; finally he was cast ashore where he thanked God with tears for saving him from an inevitable death. When a farmer asked him why he was crying Theophane told him that he wanted to settle somewhere in a desert place and live in seclusion and asked him to show him such a place. The farmer took him to a thick wood where there was a hut and Theophane settled in it.

    The Lord purifies and brings to higher perfection the chosen ones in different ways in accordance with their spiritual state. Before, Theophane had many good intentions and pious wishes, but there was no complete selflessness and obedience to God's will; he did not have the inflexible determination to lead an ascetic life. Therefore the Lord exposed him to sorrow and temptations in order to strengthen his good intention. Some people found Theophane in the hut where he had settled and took him to Kem where he was taken into custody before sending him to the Solovetsky Monastery. Seeing that his guard had fallen asleep, Theophane slipped out of the place of detention and ran to the forest. On his way he came across some travellers and asked them to show him such a desert place that nobody would find him there. The people took pity on him, put rags on him, gave him some food and took him up river about thirty km away where they showed him a trappers' hut. But the hermit was disturbed there. Some Pomor trappers found him and having learnt that he was Theophane, former agent of the Solovetsky Monastery, they thought that he had escaped from the monastery with some money and wanted to take it off him. When Theophane began to assure them that he did not have any money, the trappers burnt his hut, beat him, tortured him with fire; then tied him with a rope and pulled him under the ice in the lake from one ice-hole to another

threatening either to take him to the monastery or
to drown him in the lake. They did not achieve what
they wanted and left him half dead. Having come to
his senses Theophane thanked God for the sufferings
he had experienced admitting that he had deserved
even harder punishment for his sins. When he saw
that his hut had been burnt and the bread and tools
given by kind people had been stolen, he prayed
God with tears: "O Lord, You see my sufferings and
misfortune: I have nothing to eat and to cover my
body; I call upon Your mercy, help me. I will die here
if God wants me to; but the Lord can strengthen me".
Feeling better he went to another place, obtained
fire, gathered firewood and with great difficulty dug
a cave. Having neither bread nor tools for digging
roots, he gathered rotten wood and moss and boiled
them in water in a bowl made of birch bark, and ate
them. But this food made the hermit very weak and
he expected to die any minute. Afterwards he said
that severe hunger made him eat such food, but his
stomach refused to take it. When he swallowed it, he
felt such a severe pain that he fell on the ground and
bidding farewell to life said: "Lord, take my spirit
in peace". Then feeling some warmth inside himself
he stood up and beseeched God to strengthen him.
In such sufferings Theophane lived till summer;
then he stored up some roots, moss, various berries
and lived on this for five years. When the people
who lived nearby learned about the hermit, they
began to bring him some necessary things. When
Theophane began to sow rye and barley in a good
place that he had chosen himself, he had enough
grain to eat and could even sometimes give it to
others. His prayer rule was 2400 prostrations a
day. Many people, especially those who lived in
Kem loved Theophane as their spiritual father.
Theophane lived there for twenty-four years. The
local authorities disapproved of him teaching people

and threatened him with banishment. And soon hieromonk Joseph from the Solovetsky Monastery did come and took the hermit to the monastery. It was in 1817 when archimandrite Paisios was in charge. The elder arrived at night and came to Matins in the church of Saints Zosima and Sabbatios; he touched their relics and began to listen to the service with a deep emotion. The hermit looked very strange: he was small, black from smoke, with a dilapidated kamilavka on his head, wearing ragged clothes. Soon Theophane was allowed to leave the Solovetsky Monastery for the Golgotha Hermitage on the Anzersky Island. Pomors would come to him and complain of his leaving them; they were ready to take the elder with them. Theophane drove the tempters away. At that time the elder was seventy three years old; he was not strong enough to bring water and firewood up the mountain to his cell; so in autumn they built him a cell at the foot of the mountain and he settled there. He suffered many illnesses, people's vexations, temptations and attacks of evil spirits. Sometimes he would hear near his cell the sound of tambourines, timbals, clapping of hands, footsteps around the cell and striking on the walls and windows. When he began his prayer rule the demons' attacks would increase, but the ascetic would continue praying. His bodily needs were often satisfied by the monastery and by pilgrims' offerings. He would not refuse to give advice to the brethren coming from the monastery. "Seeking eternal blessing", he would tell the monks, "do we hope to obtain salvation without deliverance from our passions? No man can serve two masters: for either he will hate the one, and love the other; or else he will hold to the one, and despise the other. Ye cannot serve God and mammon (Mathew 6:24)". Shedding tears he would add: "Look at the sweetest Lord Jesus Christ! Saving us, how much torment, beating, humiliation and finally crucifixion did he bear? And when, being exhausted, he said: "I thirst!" What was he given? Ungrateful Jews did not give him even a drop of water, but gave him a vessel full of vinegar: and they filled a sponge with vinegar, and put it upon hyssop, and put it to his mouth. (John 19:28, 29) And we satisfy our bodily needs! Christ's ascetics did not seek comfort. For example, when Saint Paramon suffered from fever he did not give any relief to his body. And we eat and drink without a real need and do not consider it to be reprehensible. Do we not have a common meal? We have enough food and drink there: what else do we need? But we come to our cells and instead of doing the prayer rule and reading books or doing other God-pleasing work in silence we indulge in idleness, pleasing our body and satisfying our bodily needs. We call a brother or two and start idle talking, discussing what each of us saw or heard about someone; sometimes one of the brothers begins to criticize someone, and his brothers agree with him wanting to please him; the other brother may talk about wishing to buy something, to go somewhere and so the brethren corrupt each other. Is this brotherly spiritual love? No, it is not brotherly, in fact it is harmful to the soul. We had better shed tears".

To some monks he gave the following precepts: "If we renounced the world to save our soul and seek eternal good, then salvation is impossible without feats and patience, without sorrow and temptations, without hunger and thirst. Yet we are always looking for the sweet, and complain about that which is not sweet; we eat and drink excessively; we do not keep the commandments. It is not a true path; the one who did not taste the bitter cannot have the sweet. It is obvious that we have forgotten why we left the world; it would be better for us to have stayed there, than having come to the monastery and become monks, to do worldly things; it is better not to know the path of truth than to know it and to go astray; it is better not to make vows than to make them and not to keep them and to become exposed to torture. If I had made monastic vows when I was tonsured like you do now, I would not have received the complete monastic tonsure being afraid of the great responsibility. It would have been enough for me to wear a cassock and do what is appropriate with a cassock, to receive at least a small reward without the fear of being condemned. And now I see many novices bustling about to receive the monk's habit; but the one who received the tonsure promised to stay in the monastery and serve God in poverty, hunger and obedience. Soon we forget about it and live even in worse neglect than before. So let us not be like that; let each of us try to begin practising virtues; God's reward corresponds to one's labour. Let us serve God in humility and meekness; He says: "To this man will I look, even to him that is poor and of a contrite spirit, and trembleth at my word" (Isaiah 66:2). Obey without deviating the rules established by your spiritual fathers; follow the fathers' precepts and do not break the monastery rule. When you meet a brother bow to him; do not enter another monk's cell without necessity, do the assigned work of obedience with humility; avoid idleness. In church, stand with all your attention and zeal; serve the sweetest Jesus with all your heart and renounce worldly passions. Then the Lord will open the eyes of your heart, and you will see the devil's nets and drop evil passions; if you please our Lord Jesus Christ you will be able to follow our fathers Zosima and Sabbatios and, being granted Christ's grace, enter the Kingdom of Heaven.

  Two brothers asked Theophane to supervise them after their tonsure. The elder agreed and began to teach them how to lead a monastic life, and to pray for them. Once during prayer the evil spirit appeared to him and said: "Evil old man, you are praying for your disciples but in future they will not be the same as they are with you; our time will come". "God will not allow that to happen", answered Theophane. Another time, when he was praying for the same disciples, the Devil told him: "You are doing your work, and I am doing mine; I have shot two arrows at one of them and I am whispering in the other's ear". The elder became sad, he called his disciples and when they came he discovered some minor sins in them; he preached to them, gave them instructions and let them go. In the days of archimandrite Paisios there was some disturbance in the monastery. The disciples asked Theophane: "How long is this confusion going to last? And who is going to become archimandrite?" The elder answered: "Our enemy the devil is tempting our monastery and those who live in it; those who were tempted proved to be impatient. Therefore the monastery will suffer disgrace, but soon through the prayers of the Saints it will be over and it will become even more famous. There will be two superiors similar to Zosima and Sabbatios who will manage it in humility of spirit and simplicity of heart, caring for their neighbours' salvation; then many will excel in virtues".

Testing one of his disciples Theophane asked him: "How do you put together your fingers to cross yourself?" The disciple put together three fingers and said: "I do it, father, as the Orthodox Church teaches us. All over Russia obedient sons of the Church put their fingers in the same way as I do to cross themselves". Theophane said: "Living in seclusion I did not forbid simple people to cross themselves with two fingers, if only they go to church; but you should beware of the followers of the schism. When I used to live in Kiev I never saw anyone who crossed himself with two fingers. I have been to Moldavia, to the Nyamets Monastery where abba Paisios is in charge and there are seven hundred brothers from different countries: Moldavians, Serbs, Bulgarians, Hungarians, Greeks, Armenians, Jews, Turks, Russians, Ukrainians – they all crossed themselves with three fingers and had never heard about two finger crossing".

Once Theophane went to the Solovetsky Monastery to bow before the relics of the Saints and to visit his disciples. Having come to Matins the elder stood in the corner and watched the monks touching the holy relics. With his inner eyes he saw Saints Zosima and Sabbatios sitting in their shrines and blessing some monks, but turning away from others. Therefore the elder gave his disciples the precept to touch the shrines of the saints with reverence every day.

By his precepts the elder impressed on his disciples self-control and composure. In order to encourage those who were afraid of the difficulty of doing feats for the sake of salvation he said: "In our time there are also unknown hermits, true monks and Christ's anointed.

Lay people also often would come to the elder asking for precepts. He would teach them to work and not to be idle, not to complain and to go to church.

The stories of all ascetics show that the more they succeeded in subjugating their bodies and renouncing their love of the world, the more the enemy of salvation attacked them. One morning, when Theophane was doing his prayer rule, two menacing demons appeared. "You see", they cried, "the old man does not want to reform; let us destroy his cell and burn him". It seemed to the elder that they began to destroy the cell, they broke the windows and the door and cried: "Now he will not escape from us". The elder became frightened, fell to the ground asking God for help and intercession and soon the demons disappeared. Having prayed, the elder stood up and saw that his cell was safe and sound. The Lord would strengthen the ascetic in this struggle by beneficial visits. Soon afterwards in a dream the Shining Lady with two shining men appeared to him and encouraged him, persuading him not to be fainthearted and not to fear demons' attacks. The vision had not yet disappeared when a horde of demons appeared and threatened to kill the hermit. But when they saw the Lady they shuddered and yelled: "Woe is us! His Protector has come: if it were not for Her, we would have killed this monk long ago". Having said that they disappeared. This dream filled the elder's heart with hope in the Mother of God's help. Every day he would make a hundred prostrations saying the Mother of God's prayer.

Memorable are the precepts which Theophane gave his disciples, persuading them to be true monks. "My children in God", he said, "love the Lord with all your heart; serve Him with fear and love; keep His Divine commandments; mortify your flesh by temperance and work; keep the vows made at your tonsure; avoid love of the world and its pleasures; rid yourselves of bodily weaknesses and serve not your belly but God; renounce the world for the sake of the sweetest Christ; love the one God and everybody will love you; respect your brothers and you will be respected. Consider yourselves to be the most unworthy so that the Lord will raise you above your passions. Cure yourselves of pride, for the Lord "scorneth the scorners: but he giveth grace unto the lowly" (Proverbs 3:34). I beg you, my children, be attentive when you pray, so that your prayer offered to the Lord will not become a sin. When you pray do not be far away from it, do not work in vain singing psalms only with your lips and wandering with your mind around different places. Pray with fear of God, for a prayer is a conversation with God, therefore saying the words of the prayer call upon God with your entire mind. In church, stand there as if before God, saying psalms with your tongue and listening to what you hear with your mind. Remember who you are speaking to. Never be idle in your cell, for idleness harms even the zealous, particularly you, who are young. A young monk who remains idle in his cell will not avoid laziness and relaxation; at this moment the sly one suggests to him many evil thoughts and the monk cannot resist them and falls, fulfilling the enemy's will. The Holy Fathers say that the one who sits idly in his cell struggles with a multitude of demons in vain and is always beaten. The one who does the work of obedience or some manual work struggles with one demon and defeats him easily. Remember the story about the great hermit who lived with his disciple. Demons said that they could not approach the elder and never saw his disciple idle for he was constantly building and destroying. The elder was guarded by God's grace and the disciple was building a stone wall and knocking it down to avoid idleness; working in this way he resisted the enemy. My children, do pray and be vigilant with your mind as the psalm says: "I have set the LORD always before me: because he is at my right hand, I shall not be moved" (Psalm 15:8) and " Mine eyes are ever toward the LORD; for he shall pluck my feet out of the net" (Psalm 24:15).

 Glorified is my Creator, I say the Jesus Prayer in my mind without compulsion. Work when you are young and settle the sweetest Jesus in your hearts, obtaining now the Consoler, the Spirit you will be able to become joyful in your old age. If you listen to me you will see the Divine Light which will inspire you to do good deeds. I say to you, if you follow my precepts and my admonitions, then you will be with me where I am destined to be. If you ignore my words, it is not my fault because I have told you everything".

Not long before his death evil people came to Theophane looking for money; they beat him, pulled the hair off his head and beard, burnt his body with a firebrand, left him hardly alive and went away. Theophane lay half dead for three days suffering from hunger and cold; he never totally recovered of that till the end of his life. This old hermit looked very strange to visitors – without a beard or hair on his head, with a broken spine and beaten body.

But the end of his life was very close. Once light illuminated his cell and the hieroschemamonk Jesus of Golgotha appeared to him: "Rejoice, brother", he said, "soon you will pass away". He also had another vision which predicted his death, but he said with certainty that he would live till summer. The elder was not afraid of a nearing death: he wanted it to come; but sometimes he worried about the severity of Divine justice and the heights of the monastic vows. He was consoled by hope in God's mercy to repentant sinners and mourned over the weak life of some of the brethren and worried that his disciples might be tempted by bad examples. Once in a dream he saw two deceased hermits who had lived on the Muksalmsky Island. Their names were Anthony and Theodose. "May you be in peace with God, our beloved brother", they told the elder. "Do not mourn over the brethren who live in the cloister; in our time there are many temptations and attacks: those will be saved who save their soul. Your disciples are not ascetics yet; they are like the others". Theophane called his disciples and told them to intensify their fasting and prayer.

Theophane spent the winter in a very bad condition and in spring he was taken to the Solovetsky Monastery. He suffered from fever and all food seemed bitter to him.

Many visitors would come to him and this quite disturbed him. Before the Apostles' Fast when Theophane was fading away he was transported to the cell of his disciple Anthony. The elder lay in the cell for three days and in accordance with his wish received communion. Addressing his disciple Anthony he said: "So, my child, the time of my death is approaching, the hardest and the most frightful time in my life when what is concealed will be revealed, the time feared even by the righteous; it is an illness which is worse than all other illnesses, a time full of horror and fear". The elder began to look around as if frightened of someone and then asked his disciple to cense the cell. Theophane died and gave his spirit to God on July 26th 1819, being 75 years old. His remains were buried in the monastery, near the chapel dedicated to Saint Herman, in front of the icons, opposite the local icon of the Mother of God, by the Holy Doors.

Starets Nahum

Origin. – Orphaned. – Arrival at Solovetsky Island. – Admission to the monastery. - Novitiate. – Ryasophore. – Move to the Anzer Hermitage. – Banishment. – Return. – By the holy relics. – The second banishment. – Arrival at Kem. – Return to the Solovetsky Monastery. – Visit of the bishops. – Precepts. – Understanding. – A remarkable incident. – Illness

The elder Nahum, a Karelian by origin, was born in the Kemsky district of the Arkhangelsk Region, near Kamenny Lake, in the village of the same name, about 300 km from the Solovetsky Monastery. His parents, Pachomios and Maura, were simple and poor peasants. They died when Nahum was a small child. Life as an orphan became his best teacher: it prevented him from having passions which are typical of a young age, accustomed him to patience and work, formed him according to the rules of Christian morality, and put love of God into his pure soul. He was called to an ascetic life in his dreams. Afterwards he said: "In my dreams I often saw kind elders wearing monks' habits inviting me to go with them somewhere; I had never seen monks before, but when I visited a monastery, I learned what rank the mysterious visitors belonged to and where they invited me to".

Providence was leading young Nahum to the destiny determined for him. One well-to-do Karelian, Nemchinkin by surname, rented a fishery on the Solovetsky Island, near Reboldskaya wharf, 15 km away from the monastery, and every summer he would catch fish there and in winter he would return home. This man felt compassion for the homeless boy and began to take care of him. In the summer of 1791, he took Nahum to the Solovetsky Island. At that time Nahum was fourteen years old. He diligently worked for his benefactor all summer, but when winter came he did not want to return home with him for he was charmed by the beauty and silence of the monastery and longed to stay with the monks forever. Nahum was admitted to the monastery as a pilgrim and willingly began to do whatever work of obedience was assigned to him. However in summer he again was employed by his benefactor Nemchinkin who paid taxes for him, and in winter he returned to the monastery. He had to alternate monastic obedience and private trade for some years until the monastery authorities, having become certain of his capacity for an ascetic life, assumed paying taxes for him. Since then the humble young man lived quietly and serenely in the silence of the monastery.

In summer they would make Nahum, as he was experienced in trapping, catch fish at the Sosnovaya Bay, to the north of the monastery. They say that if he caught many animals he, combining the well-being of the monastery and the kindness of his kind heart, would release some animals. In winter he would work at the monastery tannery and spend his spare time learning reading and writing in Russian which he had not mastered in his childhood.

He lived many years doing this hard work of obedience without any reward or praise and even without a private cell to rest and pray. In 1801 he spent all summer on the Sekirnaya Mountain watching English ships as there was a breach of diplomatic relations with England. But he would never complain because he did not think that he deserved any attention. His main characteristics were constant peace of mind, meekness and kindness.

Experienced ascetics already considered him to be a man of high spiritual life. So the elder Theophane who had lived in seclusion for twenty five years asked upon his arrival at the monastery: "Who is Nahum here? Show him to me: he is building a beautiful palace for himself". Both ascetics would meet and talk, but the subject of their conversations remained secret.

In 1819, twenty eight years after entering the monastery, Nahum was allowed by archimandrite Paul to wear a monk's habit. The ascetic was so happy to become a monk. At that time he was working in the prosphora bakery. When in the time of archimandrite Macarios the regular reading of the Psalter was established in the Anzer Hermitage, Nahum was assigned this work of obedience and officially appointed psalm-reader, besides he was given some duties in the hermitage household. There he finally received a cell where every night he would say his prayers and make prostrations before the icon of the Mother of God. He had only two books: the Psalter which he used to read prayers and the Ladder of St. John of the Ladder which he used to learn about an ascetic life.

Nahum's life on the island was peaceful and quiet, but soon he was overtaken by a temptation which, however, contributed to his fame. Under the new superior it was discovered that Nahum lived in the monastery without permission of his village authorities; the decision was made to banish him from the monastery and send him to his official residence. Relying on Providence, without any objections, Nahum submitted to his fate and sailed home with some Pomors. The unfavorable wind made them land on Zayatsky Island. A week passed but the wind still did not change; another week passed, but the wind was the same. His fellow travellers considered the presence of Nahum to be the cause of this misfortune and decided to take him back to the monastery. So he returned to the Solovetsky Island, the wind changed and the Pomors went home. This event surprised everybody and served as an obvious indication of God's protection of Nahum and he was allowed to return to his hermitage.

The ascetic's life in the Anzer Hermitage again became quiet and peaceful. He took part in all the brethren's work and combined it with voluntary ascetic feats. As before he would retreat to pray in silence; at night he would sleep as little as possible; he would never wash in a bath-house; he would never drink wine, beer, tea and never wear warm clothes, he even had no shirt and wore just a rough under-cassock and such a worn-out outer cassock that a beggar would not take it if he found it in the street. He had the habit of bathing in the sea in summer and in winter he would quite often plunge in snow or an ice-hole without fear of falling ill.

Prayer feats made the ascetic's heart so gentle that he would always shed tears of deep emotion, especially in church during sermons. "You are crying, Nahum. Why cannot I cry?" asked a monk. "Your time will come", answered Nahum hardly restraining his tears.

At that time, however, Nahum was not yet honoured by the brethren, trying to avoid giving cause to be respected and cultivating humility in himself. Once in the evening two boats of fish were delivered to the hermitage from the fishery and everybody came to scale and salt the fish. Nahum was the last to come and the manager reproached him with laziness and threatened to banish him from the monastery. "You will leave the monastery sooner than me", replied Nahum with a smile and scaled more fish than the others. After a year the manager did leave the monastery.

In 1826 the archimandrite of the Kirillovsky Monastery of Novgorod, Dositheos, was appointed superior of the Solovetsky Monastery. He had been tonsured in Solovetsky and at the beginning of his monastic life he did the trapping and fishing together with Nahum and taught him reading and writing. When the new superior arrived at the hermitage he hardly recognized in the weak and exhausted elder wearing rags his former co-worker who had laboured humbly for the monastery for 36 years. Archimandrite Dositheos summoned him to the monastery, released him from obedience work and assigned him to read the synodicon in the church of Saints Zosima and Sabbatios and to light candles in the chapels of Saints Herman and Irenarch. Nahum performed his service by the tombs of the holy Wonder-workers of the Solovetsky Island undeviatingly for 27 years till his death, without changing his way of life in spite if his old age. The church of the Saints was not heated even in winter, but Nahum would not put on any warm clothes even during the most severe frost and would wear only his riasson and cassock. Sometimes he was told with compassion: "Father, you are cold", but he would answer with a smile: "It is all right; on the other hand I do not feel like sleeping". Being free from the general work of obedience Nahum, however, did not allow himself to be idle when free from the divine service and cell prayer. In winter he would store firewood and make wooden floats for fishing nets. His cell was always so full of these floats that there was hardly any space left to move. In summer he would work on five small vegetable plots which he had made himself and which were situated in different places: the nearest was by his cell, and the farthest was a km away from the monastery. He would labour there every day like a tireless ant, sowing barley and oats, planting various vegetables.

But he would rarely eat the fruit of his work giving everything to the brethren and the Karelians who visited the monastery. He shared his cell with a rooster and a cat; the rooster acting as a clock and, of course, it served as a symbol of vigilance and sobriety of spirit. Nahum's sleep was very short: he would never sleep in the daytime; at night, an hour before morning prayers he would wake up his neighbours by ringing a bell hanging in the hall. A wooden board about 30 cm wide served as a bed and a log was his pillow. Constantly working, Nahum did not keep long fasts, but his temperance can be called permanent fasting. He did not have any food in his cell and he would go to the refectory to have lunch and dinner every day, but he would eat very little. When white bread was given he would eat just a little bit of his portion and would give the rest to his neighbours expressing in this way his love for the brethren; almost all the brothers were happy to accept this from him.

    Thus Nahum laboured, peacefully approaching the end of his life. Providence, which sends pious people various temptations to purify their virtue tested this servant of God by a second banishment. In 1834 a population census was held and the government demanded to check the dismissal testimonies of all those who lived in the monastery. Though Nahum's dismissal testimony was in the monastery, at that time it was not found among the other documents. The monastery authorities were unwilling to start a correspondence with the government about the elder who had devotedly served there for forty years. So during the Holy Week, on Maundy Thursday, they put Nahum on a boat and sent to the town of Kem in his native district. Having arrived in Kem he did not begin settling this matter but instead went to church to attend the evening service; then he stayed a night at some house and when the bell rang came to the church again; in this way he spent the other days. After Easter he began to work to earn his living. Though his friends from the monastery had collected 20 roubles for him and given this money to the guide, Nahum did not want to use other people's property; he did not petition for the dismissal certificate either. Some citizens and merchants of Kem who knew about his piety showed concern for his situation and obtained an official document proving that he had been given permission to leave for the Solovetsky Monastery to become a monk. Two weeks later the mayor of the town took him back to the monastery. On May 9th beyond expectation, the brethren saw Nahum again in the monastery and their joy was immense. So Nahum returned to his favourite cell and his previous work. As before he would invariably go to church and nobody remembered him missing any service. Only sometimes he was late for matins and in this case he would say: "I overslept today and did not hear the church bell though I woke up the others an hour before matins". Sometimes when he worked in the distant vegetable gardens he was also late for the evening service. If someone in this case reproached him jokingly, he would reply to this friendly reproach with a smile: "Your recompense will be as small as mine, for the Lord rewards the last ones in the same way as the first ones".

Though the elder tried his best to avoid people and to be unnoticeable he was visited by many worldly people both mighty and unknown ones. Two bishops – Ignatios of Olonets and Bartholomew of Arkhangelsk – while staying in the Solovetsky Monastery often came to his cell. Once, having seen the pile of fishing floats, bishop Ignatios told the elder: "Father, you labour so much, but I spend my life in idleness and inactivity". The elder answered:

"No, Lord Bishop, you do not, your labours are great and God-pleasing; and I am particularly happy that you have started to teach our priests the Karelian language so that they can preach to our countrymen in Karelian; for few of them understand Russian. This is good; nobody did it before you". During this conversation a cock sitting behind the firewood made some noise and bishop Ignatios asked: "What do you need a cock for?" "It is very useful to live with it: when it starts crowing at night I remember the Apostle Peter who was woken up to mourn his sins by a cock's crow..." Bishop Ignatios loved the elder and came to him another time to say goodbye. Bishop Bartholomew favoured the elder and would send him prosphora and letters asking his prayers to help lead the congregation entrusted to him.

Nahum did not possess the gift of making speeches, but his simple and brief precepts based on his personal experience and filled with power and spirit made a deep impression on those who sincerely asked him for advice. "A cell is the same as a hermitage", he would tell those who lamented the eremitic silence. In fact living among people he had never been inside any other cell than his own; loving everybody equally he did not favour anyone; being concerned with his own salvation he seemed to be indifferent to everything. In such a frame of mind one can really live among people as if in seclusion.

"Read the Psalter, only the Psalter", he advised both learned and unlearned people and did not praise those who read many books. Apparently he was inspired by the great Church Fathers' teaching about the Psalter, stated in the preface of a church edition of the Book of Psalms.

To novices who could not attend church services Nahum would say: "Any diligent work done with remembrance of God is equal to church prayer; both are God-pleasing and useful for us". He would urge hired people who lived outside the monastery and worked all day long to make some prostrations and pray to God as soon as they awoke. The elder himself must have done it for the first three years of his monastic life. He would usually say to all monks and laymen who asked him how to save their souls: "Ask your conscience and listen to it, and it will set you on the path of salvation".

He would kindly greet newly-tonsured monks and urge them to drop all desires and passions of the body and the soul as soon as they were tonsured – "to keep the mind free from idle talk and slander, the belly from intemperance, the hands from evil deeds; to make the legs know only two ways: to church and to works of obedience; to guard the mind and the heart against sinful thoughts and thereby to glorify God in our soul and bodies".

Nahum considered the monastic life to be higher than the worldly life and called the former kingdom, and the latter slavery. "Monks have two kingdoms: they reign here and hope to reign after death", he exclaimed seeing monks free from worldly concerns and various temptations and causes of sins and serving God by prayer feats in a quiet refuge.

Having experienced sorrow and suffering in his life Nahum had a special gift for consoling those who were exhausted with the burden of misfortunes and temptations. "Do not mourn, brother; it is through troubles and temptations that we go to the Kingdom of Heaven". He compared sorrow to a storm which rages for some time but then is replaced by silence and quiet.

His precepts to those who suffered from lust were very instructive. For their edification Nahum would relate how he had achieved dispassionateness: "Once a woman came who wanted to talk to me; our conversation was not long, but passion took possession of me and gave me no rest day and night, and I suffered and struggled with this fierce passion not for a day or two, but for three months. I did whatever was possible. But even bathing in snow did not help. Once after performing the evening prayer rule I went outside the fence to lie in the snow. Unfortunately they locked the gate; what was I supposed to do? I ran around the fence to the other gate, the third monastery gate; it was also locked. I ran to the tannery. But nobody lived there. I was wearing only a cassock and was shivering with cold; I could hardly wait for morning and with great difficulty reached the cell more dead than alive; but still the passion did not subside. When the Christmas Lent started I went to the confessor, confessed my trouble with tears and received a penance; only after that, through God's grace I reached the desired peace".

Having purified his spirit by prayer and fasting, Nahum was honoured with visions and the gift of discernment. Once before matins he was going to the chapel of St. Herman with a lantern to light the icon-lamp and he saw the saint himself wearing a riasson and a klobuk and going from the cathedral to his chapel; Nahum followed him and entered the chapel, but did not see anybody inside. Having understood whom he had seen with his own eyes, he urged everyone to come to the tombs of the holy Wonder-workers every day and kiss their shrines. We will introduce our readers to some of Nahum's many insights.

In 1847 spring was unusually cold, and in June due to the arctic winds the sea around the Solovetsky Islands was still covered with ice; pilgrims who usually came to the monastery in the beginning of May had not yet appeared. Once, it was June 9th, during the service devoted to the Saints, archimandrite Demetrios was standing by the Saints' shrines and crying about the pilgrims' misfortune. Nahum, as was his duty, was reading the canon to the Saints. Having noticed the superior's tears he asked him quietly: "Brother, why are you crying?" "I cannot help crying", answered the archimandrite, "it is probably because of my sins that God is not giving us warmth, and pilgrims are suffering on the sea; they might become exhausted and return home without visiting the Saints". "Do not lose heart, brother", objected Nahum, and he showed him the words of the third ode in the canon to the Saints "relieve misfortunes and sorrows", and continued: "You see, they are given grace to help and save those who suffer from misfortunes; they take care of their worshippers who with faith and love aspire to reach their holy relics; you will see, tomorrow all the pilgrims will be here". And then he added: "How is the Anzer Hermitage? There is not much space there; the inn is small and there are few cells; and there may not be enough bread; we should have sent them more flour in the winter". The archimandrite listened to the elder's words in wonder, but his prediction proved correct. About two thousand pilgrims who had put out to sea from Arkhangelsk, had ice on their way and finally reached the Anzersky Island with great difficulty; there they occupied all the inns, cells and buildings of the two hermitages; there was another problem: many of the pilgrims did not have any bread; the poor food supplies of the hermitages were exhausted in two days, and it was not possible to send anyone to the monastery to fetch bread. Then a courageous man took a boat-hook and jumping from one ice-floe to another reached the Solovetsky Island and told the monastery about the sad condition of the pilgrims. This news was received in the evening of the day on which Nahum talked to the Superior. Aid was at hand immediately and the next day the pilgrims arrived at the monastery.

According to the monastery's custom young oxen given by the coastal inhabitants were released to pasture on the island for the whole summer without any cowherd. One summer Nahum came to the Superior and requested permission to look after the oxen pasturing on the island. "We take care of our bodily peace and we also should take care of the oxen; the young oxen are left without any supervision; they may easily wander into some place and die". The elder's request, however, was not satisfied. A week later the Superior met Nahum and asked: "So, shall we count the oxen?" Shaking his head the elder replied: "It is too late". What had happened? Seven of the best oxen wandered into a coastal hut where monastery workers usually rested during haymaking, fifteen km from the monastery; turning about inside they closed the door, could not get out and died there of hunger and thirst.

In 1848 the monastery authorities ordered to store the yearly supply of rye in one of the stone towers next to the mill instead of in barns behind the monastery. Nahum did not like this order. When it was executed, he suggested replacing the wooden ceiling of the tower by a brick vault. "Water may pour through the boards on the rye, and it will become unsuitable for making flour, then we will only be able to make malt from it". They thought that the elder was concerned with protecting the rye from rain; but the roof and the ceiling of the tower were in a good condition, so no danger was expected from this side. But in the same year, on a winter's night, the saw-mill situated outside the monastery near the tower caught fire, the fire spread to the tower roof and the ceiling; and when extinguishing the fire, water poured on the rye and as a result much of it had to be processed into malt.

Once a pious merchant's widow from Arkhangelsk, who was old and had an adult son and daughter came to Nahum to receive a blessing and precepts. The woman made a low bow before him. "You should bow before God instead of a Karelian", the elder told her, took three barley ears from the sheaf hanging behind the door, gave them to her and said: "Here is a blessing for you; now keep them and then when it is necessary, sow them and feed your daughters from their fruit". The pious widow who did not intend to marry again and was not pleased to hear such a counsel; however the elder's prediction came true. Twenty years later the widow became a nun and afterwards became the Mother Superior of the Shenkursky Monastery where she fed her spiritual daughters with the produce of farming.

Nahum did not live to see the bombardment of the monastery by the British and died two years before that; but he foresaw dangers and hardships threatening the cloister and predicted them in vague hints.

In the thirties when they were building wooden inns on the hills behind the monastery, Nahum said that they had better build them at the foot of the mountain so that neither storm nor lightning could damage them. One of these inns was severely damaged during the bombardment, being shot through like a sieve.

In 1848, when Russia, allied to Austria made war on Hungary, Nahum kept speaking about a war with the British. At that time even the most far-sighted politicians probably did not imagine a war in the East.

A year before his death, his concern about the protection of the monastery from some great danger increased. He began often going out to the fortification walls, even at night and would tell those whom he met: "It would be good to block these embrasures with thick bricks, and to put a stone vault instead of a wooden roof over the wall and to cover it with turf. God knows, what may happen." He explained his apprehensions: "It may thunder, it may hail, or lightning may strike, it can bring trouble".

As far as the storage of grain is concerned, he would say: "It would be good to take the grain to the forest, dig a big pit, pour the grain into it and cover it with boards and turf". Expecting another attack after the bombardment, they took the grain to the forest, just as the elder advised, and one half of it was put in the barn, the other was put in the pit.

About the cattle kept on the Muksalmsky Island, across the strait, nine km from the monastery, he would say: "You had better make a large raft and bring the cows on this island, and build a stable for them". "Why should we do that?" objected those who heard this, "the cows are much better and quieter there." "Later you can take them back there," the elder replied. So just as Nahum said, at the time of danger the cattle was taken on a large raft from the Muksalmsky Island to the Solovetsky Island.

"The British look at our cows enviously" he told some monk. These words referred to the fact that the British sailing on business past the Solovetsky Islands could see the cattle pasturing on the coast. But later events proved that the elder's words were a prediction. During the war, the British did want to use the monastery cows and sent an envoy to the monastery demanding the cattle; having been refused they shot at the Father Superior intending to influence him by threats.

About three months before his death, Nahum, coming back from vespers, stopped at the porch of the Cathedral of the Transfiguration, and turning his face to the west looked for a long time upwards as if shocked by some awful vision and then said with tears: "It will be very hot here."

Nahum would conclude his predictions of future dangers by expressing his reverent reliance on God's will and unconditional hope in His mercy: "God is merciful, and the saints will protect their monastery from any misfortunes and death".

The later generation remembers several experiences proving that Nahum could see people's secret deeds and often exposed the sinners wishing to set them on the path of repentance and reform. Once two brothers in different cells talked with another brother, among other things they condemned the Superior, blaming him for being a bad head of the monastery. The next day Nahum came to one of the monks and said: "What did you talk about in your cell yesterday evening? Did you say that our archimandrite is weak? That he cannot control the monastery? Would we do better? Do you know that there is no other power but from God?" The brother, astonished by the exposure, began to ask forgiveness. "God will forgive you" replied Nahum and went to the other monk and told him the same things. But this monk, being quick tempered felt offended by the elder's exposure and began to prove the correctness of his opinions about the Superior expressed the evening before. "Then we will see the future Superior put you in your place". The monk did not stay for a year under the new Superior and was banished from the monastery because of his obstinate character.

One of the monks related the following experience. "When I was a novice, I stole some tea from a pilgrim and remained above suspicion; but it turned out that except for God there were people who knew about my misdeed. Soon I met Nahum who addressing me merrily said blandly: "So now, brother, you drink tea and you have enough of it, but do you do it with a light heart?" The elder said that and slowly moved away from me.

During the service in the church of the Saints two young novices hid in the altar behind the icons and talked idly. Suddenly Nahum ran into the church, found the novices behind the icons, and told them: "What are you doing? Look, what smoke is coming from here; you will blacken all the icons; the Saints will punish you!"

Nahum instructed and helped those who suffered from illnesses of the soul, but he also helped those who had bodily infirmities. The monk I., a shoemaker, suffered from some eye illness and could not do anything. Nahum treated the sore eye with oil from the icon-lamp and the sight returned; till his death the monk continued doing his obedience work.

The novice M. (a hieromonk afterwards), at the beginning of his novitiate was working in the hermitage yard and was severely attacked by a wild cow; being unconscious, with a damaged head and wounds all over his face and his body he was sent to the monastery for treatment . While this misfortune was happening to the brother, Nahum said: "One should be very careful with cows; out of ignorance they can mutilate the one who looks after them". The novice M. respected Nahum very much, so as soon as he came to the monastery he went to him, and when he entered the passage where the elder's cell was situated, the elder himself came out to meet him and greeted him merrily. The elder did not even let the novice tell him about his misfortune and immediately asked: "Do you believe, brother, that God can do everything and cure you?" The novice answered affirmatively and the elder asked again: "Do you firmly and wholeheartedly believe that there is nothing impossible for God?" After the second affirmative answer Nahum poured some water into a wooden bowl, made a cross over it and gave it to the novice saying: "Drink in the name of the Father, the Son and the Holy Spirit". The novice drank it. "Drink more". The novice resolutely refused the third bowl saying: "I cannot drink any more". Then the elder poured it on his head with the following words: "In the name the Holy Trinity may you be well". The water ran from his head along his neck and his whole body and after that the novice felt completely well; soon the wounds on his head were healed and after some days he returned to his work.

At the end of this narration about the manifestation of God's grace in Nahum we will relate the event which shows the power of his prayers for those who needed his help.

The hieromonk G. from the Solovetsky Monastery was returning to the monastery from his pilgrimage with some Pomors on a boat hired in Arkhangelsk, but unfavourable winds hindered the sailing and they had to stay motionlessly at the mouth of the River Dvina. Meanwhile the day of St. Sabbatios (September 27th) was nearing and the hieromonk G. mourned at being unable to be at the monastery on this day. In the evening, a day before the celebration of the Saint's memory, standing on deck and facing the monastery he began to pray: "Holy Wonderworkers, Zosima and Sabbatios, listen to me, your servant, and help me to reach your monastery for the celebration". At the same time he remembered Nahum and addressing him mentally said with tears: "You go to the church of the Saints every day and read the canon before their holy relics; beseech them to heed my request and honour me to celebrate with you the holy day".

The night passed and in the morning he heard the helmsman order to set sail. Due to the favourable wind they sailed 300 km and in the evening of the same day hieromonk G. disembarked from the boat on the coast of the Solovetsky Island fifteen km from the monastery. Without thinking about rest he rushed to the monastery and arrived there just in time for the liturgy. "You see, brother", said Nahum greeting him in the church before the liturgy, "you came home just in time: on the holy day and for the liturgy". "Yes", replied G., "with the help of the Saints' prayers". "It is true", said the elder, "but why did you recollect me? Remember the mouth of Arkhangelsk, how did you pray there? I am earth and ashes, what prayers can I say? But do not tell anyone about it till I die; now go and pray to God and His Saints".

Like a candle burning down, Nahum was approaching the end of his earthly journey. Two years before his death he fell badly ill and did not go out of his cell for several days. "God willing", he said, "I will recover". Indeed he soon recovered and returned to his labours. As if predicting his death he told archimandrite Demetrios: "You will die before me", though the archimandrite was ten years younger than Nahum. In 1852, in August, when the archimandrite was going to Arkhangelsk, Nahum accompanied him to the quay to all the brethren's surprise. Kissing the superior for the last time, he said sadly: "I am sorry but you will have a long journey"; and looking at the ship setting sail, he said aloud: "They should have taken some boards with them; they may need them on the journey," implying, as it became clear afterwards, that they would need a coffin. Two weeks later archimandrite Demetrios died in Arkhangelsk and his body was brought to the monastery to be buried. Archimandrite Bartholomew of the Yugskaya Hermitage was appointed as the new superior; but due to the winter the communication with the mainland was interrupted and the monks did not learn that Bartholomew had refused the position. Whishing to know where he was – in the Yugskaya Hermitage or in Arkhangelsk – the brethren asked Nahum about it. The elder answered: "He has lived in Arkhangelsk for a long time, he is very tall". This prediction came true and archimandrite Alexander was appointed Superior of the Solovetsky Monastery because of Bartholomew's refusal; at that time Alexander was priest of the Solombalsky Cathedral.

1853 was the last year of Nahum's life. However, he went to church till his last days and did not cease his labours; judging by his vivacity one could never conjecture his nearing death. About four days before his death the brethren noticed that he was ill and exhausted but continued to go to church. Two days before his death he came to the vespers and lit the candle before the icon of the Most Holy Mother of God with great difficulty, telling the monk who wanted to help him: "Let me light the candle myself for the last time". After that he did not go to church any more.

Though two novices were appointed to look after him he satisfied his small needs himself. A day before his death, in the afternoon, he went to the lake, entered the water up to his chest and stood there for a long time, too weak to get back to the bank till a monk passing by helped him out of the lake and brought him to his cell. On the same day in the evening, he received holy unction and the next morning he received communion.

In the last minutes of his life he prayed quietly and indistinctly, hardly moving his lips and counting the beads with the trembling fingers of his right hand. Many monks came to bid him farewell and bowed before him silently without disturbing his last prayers.

At two o'clock in the afternoon the big bell tolled to announce to the brethren the death of their oldest brother who had laboured zealously for 62 years for his salvation. It was June 10th, 1853. All the brethren gathered to pray for the peace of his soul; there were also many pilgrims. On June 12th the liturgy and burial service were performed by the head of the monastery and the brethren as there was no archimandrite there. Before the burial service a funeral oration was delivered and both the orator and the brethren could not help crying. At all the brethren's will he was buried inside the monastery, behind the altar of the Transfiguration Cathedral, next to the burial-vault of St. Zosima – an honour granted only to Superiors. His grave was covered with a stone plate with the following words inscribed on it: "Blessed are they who die in God! The Spirit says they will rest from their labours".

It is unknown whether Nahum was tonsured or not. Once archimandrite Dositheos met him and asked: "Do you want to be tonsured and conferred the monastic habit? I intend to present a petition to the Holy Synod about your tonsure". "Am I not a monk? What am I wearing?" objected Nahum pointing at his klobuk and riassa. After that neither Dositheos nor the other superiors thought about tonsuring him. However, everyone supposed that he had been tonsured by someone in the cell and therefore he was put into the coffin in the monastic habit.

Hieromonk Matthew

Origin. – Life in the world. – Admission to the monastery. – Sexton. – Priesthood. – Treasurer. – Cell occupations. – Schema. – Illness. – Death

Matthew was born in 1777 in a merchant family in the city of Vologda. He entered the Solovetsky Monastery when he was forty five years old. But even living in the world he led a pious life and was celibate; he liked receiving travellers and asking them about holy cloisters and monastic asceticism. He was a merchant but never missed church services; at the first stroke of the church bell he would lock up his shop and go to church. His honesty devoid of any bribery was known even to inhabitants of remote villages and they would patiently wait for him coming from church to buy the necessary things from him. "When Matthew comes back from church we will buy whatever we need from him on the square", people would say.

He served as a churchwarden for many years and learned perfectly the church rules so he knew every service by heart. When he was admitted to the monastery, at first he had the obedience of sexton, then, being experienced in trade, he was appointed a buyer; when he became a priest he also was given the position of treasurer which he held for ten years. He accustomed himself to continence when he was young, he never drank wine and tea and never washed in a bath-house; he had a meal once a day and always in the refectory. He never missed any church services even when he became old; he would come to church at the beginning of the service and would never leave until it was over; he would never sit down during the reading of kathismas in spite of the monastery customs. Because of standing for long periods both in the church and in the cell his legs were swollen and their wounds never healed. For this reason he could not wear any boots and wore loose shoes instead, but he never treated his legs and did not tell anyone about his illness. In his cell he would constantly read religious literature and copy those texts which he considered noteworthy. In his own hand, he copied many books concerning asceticism which were not published at that time. These books are still used by those who seek salvation. He followed the cell prayer rule precisely and had a habit of devoting the night to reading the Gospel. He was always filled with pious feelings and looked kindly; during church services he would stand with bowed head listening attentively to the reading and singing.

Matthew zealously obeyed the church rules and would persuade those who sang and read to perform services precisely and properly.

All superiors respected him and turned to his experience and wisdom for help; the brethren considered him to be a model of asceticism. In 1849 he was tonsured in the schema and ceased being a priest; he began to receive communion with all the brethren before the altar; he did not even bless anyone as a priest. Being fond of choral singing he attended services at the cathedral; he did not find their duration hard to bear, on the contrary he liked that. Some years before his death he lost the sight in one eye, and as a result he could not copy books and began to make woollen rosaries for brethren and pilgrims, to avoid idleness. He had never resorted to the brethren's services in his life and prayed God not to trouble anyone when nearing death – his wish came true. Two days before his death he attended the morning service at the cathedral but became extremely exhausted and left the church before the end of the service. The next day the brethren came to his cell to administer holy unction to him. "I have already received unction", said the elder seeing the preparations for unction. "Who administered unction to you?" "Young hieromonks from the cathedral came some time ago and administered unction to me". "We will also administer unction to you, for this mystery can be repeated", the brethren said and administered unction to him. The elder still could stand. Preparing to receive communion in the morning, he did not allow his disciple, the monk Palladios, to stay for the night in his cell, wishing to say the prayers before communion alone without any witnesses, but in the morning he was found lying before the lectern dressed in a stole. Standing with awe he received communion and a few hours later passed away with peace in God, on September 25th 1857, being eighty two years old.

Schemamonk Gerasim

Origin and life in the world. – Retreat to the Nikandrov Hermitage. – Wandering around holy places. – Arrival at the Solovetsky Monastery. – Eremitical life. – Staying at the monastery. – Death

George was born and lived in the town of Karachev in Orlovskaya province, and had a wife and children. Having become a widower he went to the forests of Bryansk to the elder Arsenios who had come from Athos. Soon the two hermits moved to the district of Pskov, to the Nikandrov cloister. There George was tonsured a monk with the name Gerasim. Having buried his spiritual teacher, Gerasim lived alone fasting and praying.

Because of his total devotion to God he was honoured to experience wonderful manifestations of the Divine Providence which gives whatever is needed to those who seek nothing except the Kingdom of Heaven. Once he ran out of bread and having stayed without any food for twelve days Gerasim wanted to go to the nearest village to find some food, but in the morning at the door of his cell he found a barley loaf, big and warm, and enough for him for a long time. His shirt was worn out and not having another one he stayed naked for a long time, but once he found near his cell some linen which was long enough for him to make a shirt. He suffered much from demons who wanted to try his patience by various apparitions, but he dispelled the demons' forces by the Jesus Prayer and psalms; by reading the Acathist to the Most Holy Mother of God he banished despondency and despair. He left his hermit's cell twice and travelled around the holy places of Russia : he visited Kiev, Pochaev, Nihvin and even stayed for some time in two monasteries (the Arzamassky and the Dymsky monasteries), but being unable to have peace of spirit there and longing for total silence, he returned to his secluded life. In 1823 Gerasim arrived at the Solovetsky monastery at the time of archimandrite Macarios and as a spiritual man, experienced in the eremitic life he was given the blessing to live in seclusion. At first he lived for five years in a cave ten km away from the monastery, living off a handful of dry bread and praying unceasingly. Then, because of the brethren's wish to talk to him and also due to his old age, he was moved to a newly-built cell closer to the monastery. When two years later this cell burnt down, he settled with his disciple Pamfilios in the Fillipovsky Hermitage, where the Church of the Vivifying Source is now situated. The teacher and his disciple followed the path of spiritual perfection together by praying and making small containers for salted herrings. In 1845, because of weakness and bad eyesight Gerasim was moved to the monastery hospital. He was led like a child to the divine service which he did not want to miss. At that time he was over a hundred years old, but he had a good memory and it was pleasant to talk to him as with a guest from another world who remembered the days of the reign of Empress Elizabeth Petrovna. His stories about the ascetic life were very instructive and simple at the same time and consisted of brief sayings imbued with a particular spirituality. During the last days of his life, the elder seemed to be as a child again; he did not care whether he was wearing clothes or was naked, forgetting the time of day he asked in the evening whether the matins were over, and in the morning whether the vespers had begun; but he prayed till the end of his life. Sometimes during a conversation with brethren he would suddenly stop and begin to say the Jesus Prayer. On

October 28th 1848, Gerasim passed away, in peace with God, being hundred and eight years old.

The Monk Pamfilios

*Eremitic life. – Experience of obedience. – Feats.
– Visions. – Life in the Monastery. – Second sight. –
Death*

The elder Gerasim, in his disciple Pamfilios, trained a monk who surpassed even his teacher as far as his spiritual achievements are concerned. Pamfilios worked in the monastery as a cooper and wheelman. Having committed himself to unconditional obedience to his elder, he piously kept the vow of obedience for his entire life and never did anything without his teacher's blessing. But impediments and errors are inevitable in everybody's life. Once he received a leather belt with an iron buckle without asking the elder's permission. The elder was offended by his disciple's self-will and seeing him pleased with the acquired belt he took it off him and gave him a thick rope for girding himself with instead; the obedient disciple wore the rope for about twenty years till his death. For many years Pamfilios lived with Gerasim in seclusion making small barrels; if he sometimes did not manage to do the elder's assignment, the elder deprived him of dinner on that day.

His praying feats were great. Having enlightened his inner eyes by prayer he could see with his physical eyes supernatural phenomena. He repeatedly saw the appearance of a church at the place where now the Church of the Vivifying Source is situated and told his elder about it. Sometimes, on dark nights, he saw an unusual light illuminating the surroundings of their hermitage. But he was forbidden to pay attention to such visions so as not to be seduced by spiritual pride. These wise warnings were not in vain. Once at night while he was praying, he was shocked by a terrible vision and either because of demonic violence or just fear, he lost consciousness and in the morning he was found lying on the floor unconscious. "I saw a man with fiery eyes standing by the window and breathing out flames; he asked to let him stay for the night and then the cell became full of black ravens that were flying with loud croaking sounds around me". Since then he lost the sight in one eye and his face became distorted. Pamfilios stopped living in seclusion and began to live mostly in the monastery doing the usual hand-work; sometimes he spent the nights praying and crying, and his sobbing woke up his neighbours; at midnight he went to the refectory and there continued to pray before the icon of the Mother of God of Tikhvin till matins. Always silent and concentrated on prayer, Pamfilios had a spiritual liking and respect for a fool in Christ, the woman called Christina, who often visited the monastery. Once he went to the quay telling those whom he met: "Christina is coming and I am going to meet her". And Christina, being far from the monastery, announced to the people who were in the boat with her that they would be met by a monk. The friends met on the coast with mutual respect and kissed each other on the shoulders. Till his death he kept consulting his elder, confiding him the secrets of his conscience and asking for instructions in difficult situations. His entire life was a constant feat of prayer and labour. He passed away before his elder, on September 8th 1845. When he died his face to everyone's surprise was no longer distorted and became beautiful and joyful.

Schemamonk Zosima

Life in the monastery. – Indifference to money. – Feats. – Death

The entire monastic life of Zosima, who came from the tribe of the Chuds, passed in tireless labours, strict temperance and exemplary indifference to money. Living in the monastery he never had money in his hands and did not receive small sums of money given to monks for their cell needs. The head of the Golgotha Hermitage wanted to test the firmness of his vow – not to touch money – and ordered to put a handful of copper and silver coins on the path which Zosima had to follow to come to the hermitage for the holiday vigil. Having seen the money Zosima turned off the path and stuck in the bog. He considered this experience to be a demonic temptation and preferred to become dirty in the bog rather than to touch the hateful metal. Then two tempters came out of their ambush and explained the matter. "I did not know that", answered the simple-hearted Zosima, "otherwise I would have thrown your money in the bog". There was nothing unnecessary in the monk's cell; in addition to his cassock and klobuk he had only two garments – a plain short fur coat to wear in winter and a gray caftan to wear in summer. So, leaving his cell, Zosima took all his possessions like a bird that does not leave anything behind when it moves to another place. During all his forty-seven years in the monastery he did the fishing and trapping at the Troitskaya and Kirillovskaya fisheries in summer and made nets in winter. He would often spend nights praying and crying. Knowing about his night vigil the brethren would ask him to wake them up at a certain time and he would fulfil their requests willingly and without fail though there was no clock in his cell. Before his death he fell ill and renounced the schema so that upon recovery he could pick up his usual labours for the welfare of the cloister. He died the next year after the bombardment of the monastery by the British when the monks were not yet protected from the enemy's attacks. Dying, the elder urged the brethren not to give way to cowardice in the face of danger, assuring them that through the Saints' prayers God would not let the holy place be damaged any more. All the belongings he left behind, consisted of a belt. Schemamonk Zosima died on June 23rd 1855.

Hieroschemamonk Jerome

Life in the world. – Admission to the Chutyn Monastery. – Hieromonk. – Service at the Synodal House of Moscow. – Stay at the Chernomorsky Nikolaevsky Hermitage and in Novgorod. – Imprisonment in the Peter and Paul fortress. – Exile to the Solovetsky Monastery. – Death. – Teachings on priesthood, Philokalia, schema, prayer

Jerome, in the world Hierotheos Lukin, at first was in public service from 1782 to 1795, then entered the Chutyn Monastery of Novgorod where in 1799 he was tonsured. He was ordained a hieromonk in 1808 in the Novospassky Monastery of Moscow and after that served at the Synodal House of Moscow. During the invasion of the French Jerome participated in the removal of the patriarchal sacristy from Moscow, he left the city with it and did not have time to save his property. When the war was over he moved to the Chernomorsky Nikolaevsky Hermitage in the eparchy of Novgorod. Knowing Photios well, later archimandrite of the Yurevsky Monastery, and at that time a teacher of religion in a military school, Jerome learned from him about the spread of Masonry and teachings contrary to Orthodox Christianity in society and decided to inform the government about it. For this report he was sent to the Peter and Paul Fortress from which in 1830 he was moved to the Solovetsky Monastery and was kept there under strict surveillance. Jerome received the news about his leaving the prison of the Peter and Paul Fortress with tears. "Why are you crying?" the superintendent asked. "For me, that was the best place for an ascetic feat", answered the prisoner.

Though Jerome had not studied at schools, he was a man of great intelligence and educated himself by spiritual reading and conversations with spiritual elders he happened to meet in his life. He had a gift for speaking and a rare power of persuasion; his advice was especially useful for those who suffered from evil thoughts and felt pangs of conscience. His precepts, based on his experience, were true spiritual healing. On the last days of his life he made a daily record of his thoughts, which presents many interesting psychological facts. Hieroschemamonk Jerome passed away in peace with God in the Anzer Hermitage on September 23rd 1847, being eighty two years old.

Extracts from the elder Jerome's manuscripts presented below will acquaint the reader with his ideas and his manner of speech.

On priesthood

In the old days monks led a silent and secluded life; therefore hieromonks are rarely mentioned in patericons. Nowadays there are many hieromonks in cloisters and some of them regret being deprived of the silence they used to practice. I repeatedly talked about it with experienced fathers and heard the following from them: monks who lived in silence and seclusion received consolation for their souls through the Jesus Prayer done by the mind in the heart under the supervision of experienced teachers; some monks practising this prayer fell in the devil's delusion because of their inexperience and self-will, as a result they became incurably ill. Monks who are priests are not exposed to delusion: for consecration through the sacraments is devoid of delusion and effective for those who receive them with faith. The fathers also told me that the reward granted by God to a monk diligently serving as a priest is great. Therefore the fathers say not to grieve at not practising silence like the old hermits did, but to thank God who honoured you to be priests. Your aim is the same as theirs: moral perfection. They performed their ascension in their hearts, you do it in God's churches. They moved from strength to strength – from the strength of acting to the strength of vision. You also should follow the same path: from the strength of faith to the strength of vision. It is written: "They go from strength to strength, every one of them in Zion appeareth before God" (Psalms 83:7). Those monks had Zion in their hearts; you have Zion in the church on the altar. Here you will see with your mental eye the entire Holy Trinity in the divine service: the Father receiving holy gifts, the Son giving them, the Holy Spirit creating them. So, friend, when you stand at the altar celebrating a service do not fly mentally to the clouds seeking God. He is before you now and will be forever. You will be honoured to see God when on earth you live a heavenly life. Here on earth, hieromonk, is a reward for you, judge about the future reward by this one.

On the Philokalia

Can you find a man who is able to teach you to converse with Jesus in your heart better than the Philokalia teaches you? Hardly any of the wisest men nowadays can cope with this task. It is sad to live without God. Jesus said: "For without me ye can do nothing" (John 15:5). Hence He announced His will to us: to be with Him inseparably. Therefore the Holy Fathers left in the Philokalia instructions for us on how to unite with God by keeping the mind in the heart. Though in some monastery libraries there are some excerpts from the teachings of these Holy Fathers made before the publication of the Philokalia, they are very brief. Before the Philokalia was published those who wanted to learn the Jesus Prayer would go to the Nyamets Monastery in Moldavia, to the true teacher of the Jesus Prayer, the elder Paisius Velichkovsky and having received there proper precepts they lived according to them in Russia. I have seen such people. Now that the Philokalia is published, those who want to practice diligently the prayer of the heart have an opportunity to do it, for all the devil's crafty designs are explained there. The prayer of the heart is God's gift, and not a human trick. Visiting experienced practitioners of the Jesus prayer, I saw them praying and I believe and sincerely announce that this is good for the soul, but it requires total silence. And people who occupy themselves with some troublesome work are deprived of this. First, as the experienced elders told me, one should say the prayer orally with the help of a rosary, for example, a hundred times a day being alone in the cell, so that one can listen attentively to the words of the prayer, thereby the prayer will impress itself on the memory. At the same time one should avoid any thoughts or dreams; if you cannot manage to do a hundred prayers without thoughts, you should start again from the very beginning and try to do it again without any thoughts. "This is our ABC; we all begin from there", said the elders. And if you learn to do it, you can say the prayer more that a hundred times without any thoughts. I followed these elders' instructions and have been practising the prayer of the heart for about forty years. And I thank the Lord Jesus Christ for this lesson.

    Those who practise the Jesus Prayer do not neglect church services. They are the first to come to church and the last to leave it. Only self-willed monks neglect church services. I prefer to say only one "Lord have mercy" in church than to read the entire Psalter in the cell.

On the schema

A monk's habit is a precondition for the schema. Hence every monk who has a monk's habit can be tonsured to the schema. But the true understanding of the schema has almost disappeared. Many monks do not want to receive the schema because they are afraid of the great rule concerning eating, drinking and making prostrations. But this lack of understanding should be repaired by reasoning. The schema is a total renunciation of a worldly life, that is, it consists in a monk practicing the Jesus Prayer in his heart, alone and in silence. The schemamonk should have light food and drink so as not to fall ill; he can and should make as many prostrations as he can with God's help, but not according to an assigned number. If the schemamonk is not versed in holy scriptures, he should practice reading sacred books and patericons, but not let the mind wander because of it. When God gives the ascetic a spiritual prayer, performed in the heart, then he should not cease it until it ceases of itself, and he should say it humbly without doing anything else at the same time. The schemamonk is a true and literal follower of the commandment – to love God with his whole heart, mind, and body, with all his thoughts and with his whole soul. The schemamonk can be compared to a seraph as far as the depth of his love of God is concerned. Nowadays they make the schemamonk do things which are not appropriate to him (sell candles, collect money, pray and celebrate services, stand there where lay people will see him). The master dealing with gold and diamonds is given iron pincers and a hammer and forced to forge nails. The schemamonk is a receptacle of the Holy

Spirit, an owner of many spiritual gifts, a pillar of the Orthodox Christian faith, a living human copy of the Lord Jesus Christ. Do not think that I am partial to the schema and for that reason think highly of it – it is high indeed.

When the grace of the Spirit is settled in the heart it will make it wise, better than any education will. If someone, after receiving an education, can obtain the grace of the Spirit, he can become the wisest of the wisest, such as the Apostle Paul, John Chrysostom, or Basil the Great.

On prayer

Many people filled with passions try to obtain grace from the Jesus Prayer. If a barrel was used to keep tar, will anyone agree to pour aromatic oil into it as soon as it is emptied of the tar? So can the heart in which passions resided or still reside, take the grace of the Holy Spirit? Therefore let us try first to clear the heart of the tar of passions and then we can hope to receiving the better part.

Before starting the Jesus Prayer you should ask God to forgive your sins and mortify your anger and lust. Then God Himself will teach you the prayer of the heart. Prayer of the heart is God's gift granted to His beloved servants; one in thousand is honoured to receive it. I think that the Jesus Prayer alone, without keeping the commandments cannot work. How can some people consider themselves to be men of prayer and teach others the Jesus Prayer without keeping the Lord's commandments? One more thing: the most holy name (Jesus) should be often said orally. A temple should be built starting from the foundation but not from the roof. It is written: whip milk and you will obtain butter. That is: say the Jesus Prayer orally as long as possible and your heart will begin to say it on its own. Love the quantity and you will have the quality; that is: after a long practice of oral prayer you will obtain prayer in the heart. The one who at first teaches or learns to say the prayer in the heart, must be unable to say it orally. God's grace comes unpredictably. Sometimes grace is granted to the ascetic at the beginning of his feat and sometimes at the end of his life.

There are many records in the books of the Solovetsky and Anzersky monasteries. They prove that there were monks who practiced the Jesus Prayer here before. Now these records are kept in libraries.

Do not think that now there are no people who are honoured by the gift of prayer of the heart. In the Gorokhovsky Nikolaevsky Monastery lived the monk Father Ambrose, a disciple of Paisios of Moldavia. Ambrose had a friend, an icon painter called Athanasios, who lived in a village, not far from the monastery. Once Ambrose was spending the night in Athanasios' yard. At night Athanasios went out of the house to the yard and saw Ambrose on his knees, praying; his face was shining with unusual light. Athanasios was shocked; when Ambrose noticed him he cried: "Do not believe, do not believe: it is delusion"; then he told Athanasios not to tell anyone. I heard it from Athanasios himself. At the monastery Ambrose had an associate, Athanasios by name, who also was Paisios' disciple and had the same grace.

I do not think it necessary to speak about the God-pleasing life of the schemamonk Basilisk of Valaam. Basilisk was introduced to metropolitan Gabriel who wanted to see him.

In Moscow I knew a simple man, Grigori Fyodorovich called Gonchar. He was acquainted with metropolitan Platon and enjoyed his favour. Once speaking about salvation Gonchar told the metropolitan: "Teach me how to pray". Platon told

him to say the Jesus Prayer. Gonchar followed
his advice and began to say the Jesus prayer
and then asked Platon for further instructions.
The metropolitan sent him to the Peshnoshsky
Monastery, to hieromonk Samuel. Gonchar came
to him, asked for instructions and returned home
keeping silence; he stopped doing household chores,
built a small room in his house, put there an icon
with an icon-lamp and began to practice silence. He
attended church though and was a churchwarden
till his death. For his humility and mercy towards
beggars God revealed him his nearing death.

    I also knew the monk Patermoutios form the
Otensky Monastery of Novgorod who practised
silence and the prayer of the heart. He had lived
in the monastery while there were few visitors;
when a broad road was built there from Novgorod,
Patermoutios left the monastery and began to lead
the life of a 'fool in Christ'. Metropolitan Gabriel
respected him and therefore allowed him to stay
wherever he wanted. And he lived in Novgorod
and in St. Petersburg and would often pray near
churches. He would wear rags; I saw him sitting
at a crossroads with several coins in his hand and
begging; but he usually gave beggars whatever
he received. Once I saw him in the Chutynsky
Orekhovsky garden sitting there for three days
and being badly bitten by mosquitoes. He had not
spoken to anyone for thirty years. He knew very well
the holy scriptures and the Patericons and had a gift
of understanding and reasoning. When someone
asked him sincerely and with faith, he answered by
miming and his answers proved right. He died and
was buried in the Nevskaya Lavra.

    I also know some present God-pleasing ascetics
who practice the Jesus Prayer; but the One who sees
through hearts and bodies and counts stars knows
and sees them better than me.

Schemamonk Nikodemos

Arrival at the monastery – Being a sexton – Seclusion – Feats – Schema – Death

After having become a widower Nikodemos sent his only daughter to a convent and went to the Solovetsky monastery. There he laboured zealously and cheerfully, doing many kinds of obedience work; he was the chief manager of the prosphora bakery for a long time and after that he was appointed a sexton at the hospital church. But his soul longed for a life in seclusion and silence. Having served for some time as a sexton, on the first day of Great Lent, early in morning, he escaped from the monastery. Soon the place where he was became known but archimandrite Demetrios did not allow his seclusion to be disturbed because of the general fast. A week later, however, he summoned Nikodemos to the monastery and, for leaving without permission, as penance, made him wear chains and make prostrations in church for a whole week, and then, in order to satisfy his aspiration to a secluded life the archimandrite blessed him and let him go. Nikodemos' cell was located four km from the monastery, amidst the mountains in a deep dell. He dug a well and made a vegetable garden near his cell. He lived there fasting and praying, wore chains, and ate dry bread soaked in water; he had boiled food only on holidays and had no butter at all. During Great Lent Nikodemos intensified his prayer rule and read all the four Gospels every day. Except for making prostrations in order to exert his body, he would pray for a long time standing and spreading his arms in the form of Jesus' cross, and he instructed his comrade who lived in another secluded place in this feat. In order to remember death constantly he made a coffin and put it in front of the cell. He received all visitors in a kind and friendly way and, according to the commandment of hospitality, treated them to potatoes and berries. Having lived in seclusion for seventeen years, Nikodemos caught a cold and was taken to the monastery where, upon being tonsured to the schema, he ended his ascetic life on November 3rd 1854.

Schemamonk John

Origin – Admission to the monastery – Schema – Life in St.Philip's hermitage – Feats – Death

Schemamonk John came from free peasants of the Pskov province. He served his worldly master honestly and zealously and accompanied him everywhere during a hard period of the wars between Russia and Napoleon I. Having received his liberty as a proper reward for his zealous service, he totally devoted himself to serving God by accomplishing ascetic feats. In 1827, being fifty two years old, he entered the Solovetsky Monastery and as a skilled tailor did his work of obedience as a cutter for a long time and then served as a clothes-keeper. In 1842 he was tonsured to the schema and since then for more then twenty years he lived in St Philip's hermitage in strict asceticism, silence and prayer. He celebrated the daily service in the church manner adding the monastic rule which consisted of three kathismas of the Psalter and three hundred prostrations; he never ceased to do his manual work for the brethren's welfare; he came to the monastery for certain feasts to receive communion. He suffered from various delusions and attacks from demons during his nightly prayers. He was a sincere friend of the hermit Nikodemos and they often visited each other to encourage each other in their feats. He spent the last years of his life in the monastery hospital, but even there he did not abandon his secluded way of life, so he was rarely seen in the monastery, even in the passage near his cell; but he steadily attended church services in spite of his old age almost till his death. He was approaching his death peacefully and quite painlessly, slowly and imperceptibly dying out like an icon-lamp that runs out of oil. Schemamonk John passed away in God on May 26th 1870, being ninety five years old.

Schemamonk Theodore

Origin – Tonsure – Life in seclusion – Feats – Temptation – Death

First Theodore served in the army, in the Preobrazhensky regiment. But his heart longed to serve the King of Heaven as a monk. Once he saw the Tsar and in the simplicity of his soul told him about his sincere wish to be a monk in the Solovetsky Monastery. The Tsar listened to his request but did not say anything and continued walking. Two days later the adjutant handed Theodore twenty five roubles from the tsar for a journey to the Solovetsky Monastery and ordered him to the regiment's office to receive his dismissal. We can imagine how happy he was about such an unexpected outcome! Theodore rushed to the Solovetsky Island where he was lovingly received and soon he was honoured by being tonsured with the name Philip. But the monastery life among many people did not correspond to his ardent aspirations; so Philip, having asked the superiors' blessing, settled in a secluded place where he devoted himself to eremitic feats. Fasting and night vigils were his constant occupations; the bread he made himself consisted of mashed cowberries and flour. First Philip lived on the Zayatsky Island by the church of the Apostle Andrew the First Called, a wild and gloomy place; then he moved to the Anzersky Island to the Hermitage of St. Eleazar. He suffered from many attacks of evil spirits especially on the Zayatsky Island. Once, on a dark night, when he was praying, he heard loud and hard knocks on the window. Worried by this unexpected visit the hermit went out of the cell praying, thinking he would meet someone who had landed on the island, but he did not see anyone. Many times he heard the closed door opening with a creaking sound and someone entering the inner porch, going up the stairs to the tower, walking about, knocking and coming back down. First the hermit paid attention to such incidents; but having understood that it was a demonic delusion, he continued his prayers without confusion. Once, living in seclusion on the Anzersky Island, during the night prayer he again heard knocking at the front of his cell. He went out of the cell and saw a stranger who to the question: "Who are you and what are you doing here?" responded: "I am a worker from the monastery and I am trimming an axe-handle". "Is this the right place to do it?" the hermit asked him, "May Christ be with you", and with these words the apparition disappeared. Having reached old age, Philip ceased his seclusion and came to the Anzer Hermitage where he passed away in peace.

Schemamonks Adam and Andrew

Gentleness of Adam – Fishing – Death – Andrew – Vision before death – Death

The schemamonk Adam was a paragon of simplicity and gentleness; these are the qualities of those to whom the Lord promised the Kingdom of Heaven. He was never seen being angry or criticising someone's faults and sins. He did the fishing and made nets in his cell. When there was not enough fish for the brethren Adam grieved and mourned and punished himself by depriving himself of food. He never missed any church services and never sat down in church. He could not read and write but nourished his heart and mind with the Jesus Prayer; he was fond of listening to the Lives of Saints and did his best to imitate them. Adam died in 1859, being eighty six years old. When he was a young monk his mentor was his uncle, the schemamonk Andrew, a strict ascetic who is hardly remembered nowadays. During the last minutes of his life the satan and his horde, boiling with anger and rage, surrounded Andrew's bed to confuse the ascetic and make him doubt in God's mercy. "Oh, how many of these evil creatures are crowding here ", exclaimed the elder seeing his cell crowded with dark visitors; but at the same time he received divine help and protection, and the evil spirits disappeared. "Frightened by the Queen of Heaven they have run away", he said joyfully. After that he sang with a trembling voice the hymn for the dead: "With the Saints give rest...our funeral dirge" and with the triumphant "alleluia" passed away.

Schemamonks Hilarion and Matthew

Hilarion's life in seclusion and in the monastery – Matthew's life at the hermitage – Death in the monastery

We cannot help mentioning these two bright stars of monastic asceticism. The former ascetic descended from the clergy, and after many kinds of obedience work he spent much time in seclusion; but then he considered that it was good for him to live silently in the monastery. He followed the rule not to eat for three days a week; kept total silence, concealing his feats from everybody and knowing only the church which was close to his cell. Matthew, upon being tonsured to the schema, lived at the Golgotha-Crucifixion Hermitage, constantly praying and labouring; he had a gift for weeping, and at night his sobbing was heard in adjacent cells; he never missed church services and when there was a strong wind and thick snow he crawled to church. When dying in the monastery hospital, he saw Angels at his bed. "Two Angels are standing here", he told the confessor who was there, and to the question: "What are they doing?" answered: "They are talking about something to each other". Both ascetics died very old.

The Monk Michael

Distinguishing features – Being a blacksmith – Death

The monk Michael was noted for diligence, humility and silence. For his entire monastery life, which lasted for twenty four years he stood with a hammer by the forge chimney, being the head of the blacksmiths; performing his work of obedience zealously and patiently, he cleansed his soul and made himself a God-pleasing vessel. At first he did not have a cell and lived in the forge by the forge chimney, in an alcove which was not big enough even to stretch in. Having obtained a cell, he did not have any unnecessary and even necessary things – his bed was just a plain board. Michael always kept strict silence though he was in the company of many people every day. He did not like to reprove or reprimand his subordinates, but he urged everyone to do their duty by his own example. He did not have any friends and did not visit the other cells; out of humility he never had meals with other brethren at the refectory but was satisfied with whatever he was given by refectory workers, being refused he did not demand anything and ate only some bread. Having no opportunity to attend the liturgy on ordinary days, Michael never missed the morning service and in the evening at the first stroke of the church bell he dropped his hammer and rushed to church and stood, not among the brethren, but among the workers. Because of fasting and hard labour he was very thin; in his cell he secretly kept chains in which he probably did his night prayers. A year before his death Michael wished to be tonsured to the schema or retire to a secluded place to perform prayer feats before entering eternity, but it was refused because of his young age; he received this refusal as God's will. "I must have no vocation for that", he said, staying before the forge chimney where God soon called him from temporary labours to an eternal rest. On June 23rd 1853, he passed away in peace, being forty eight years old.

Novice John Sorokin

Origin – Escape from native land – Life in the schismatic sect – Exile to the Solovetsky Island – Remarkable dream – Conversion to Orthodoxy – Death

We will conclude the narration about the lives of true ascetics by the recollection of the elder-child who lived on earth for seventy eight years, but considered that his life lasted only thirty eight days. John Vasilyevich Sorokin, a state peasant of the Kaluga province, was born and brought up in the schismatic sect. Having escaped from his native land, he spent most of his life abroad, in the Byelookrinitsky schism sanctuary where he was tonsured a monk with the name Heracles. When he went back to his native country to see his relatives, he was arrested and sent to the Solovetsky Monastery to be kept under the strictest surveillance and brought to reason and reformed. He lived on the Solovetsky Island for ten years abiding in his beliefs and wishing to end his life without repenting. But the All Good God, not wishing his son to die as a sinner, found this lost sheep and brought it to the holy Church. Having refused to read books condemning the schism for a long time, he once read about the journey of the monk Parthenios who was schismatic but then converted to the Orthodox Church; this reading aroused some doubt in his beliefs. He began to pray God to make him understand where the truth was. "One morning", he related, "after the cell prayer in which I asked God with tears: "Lord, tell me the way I should follow"; I fell asleep and dreamt that I was in some splendid palace and I heard a voice coming from above:

"Go to the Church for it is impossible to be saved outside the Church". I answered: "There are many temptations and tares in the Church". The voice said: "Why should you worry about that? You will be more special than wheat". I said: "There is a Church with a bishop and clergy in Austria". The voice replied: "The Austrian Church is not a true church, because it separated from the Eastern Church, and there is no salvation in it". That was the end of this remarkable dream and John who had never been to a church, came to a church service on January 5th, on the eve of Theophany.

The solemnity of Vespers and the Divine Liturgy of St. Basil the Great, the majestic rite of the blessing of water with glorification of the Tsar, the Synod and all Orthodox Christians, many reverent priests and the harmonious singing of the monks: all this impressed John's soul very much and he became certain that it is in the Orthodox Church that true grace resides which the blind sought in vain in the Byelookrinitsky pseudo-hierarchy. After that John went to church every day, repenting with tears of his mistakes, and on April 17th 1860, with the permission of the Most Holy Synod he joined the Orthodox Church and was included in the rank of senior novices wearing a monk's habit. But even after having joined the Church he did not stop crossing himself with two fingers. Constantly being reprimanded for this by his spiritual father he began to pray God with sincere faith and hope, to give him a sign about the truth of crossing oneself with three fingers as accepted in the Church; and once at night when John was praying he clearly heard the voice: "Believe whatever you are told : you are told the truth". Immediately, with ineffable joy, he put three fingers together and crossed himself. Since then he became a true son of the Church and it was what God's grace seemed to be expecting, because